The life of Sir Richard Fanshawe

Herbert Charles Fanshawe (1852 - 1923)

Frontispiece of The History of the Fanshawe Family (1927)

The life of Sir Richard Fanshawe 1608 - 1666

an extract from The History of the Fanshawe family (first published 1927)

H.C. Fanshawe

Valence House Publications

Published in 2016 by Valence House Publications
Valence House, Becontree Avenue
Dagenham, Essex RM8 3HT

www.valencehousecollections.co.uk

ISBN 978-1-911391-00-5

The main text is a facsimile reprint of of chapter VI of The History of the Fanshawe family by H.C. Fanshawe, published by Andrew Reid & Company in 1927

Front cover image: Sir Richard Fanshawe by William Dobson (Valence House Museum)

Cover background: details from the coronation procession of Charles II. Sir Richard Fanshawe is the right-hand figure on the back cover, acting as proxy for the absent Duke of Aquitaine. (Image from The Entertainment of his most excellent Majestie Charles II in his passage through the City of London to his coronation, by John Ogilby, 1662. LBBD Archives and Local Studies Centre, Valence House)

Illustrations

The Descendants of Fanshawe Gate

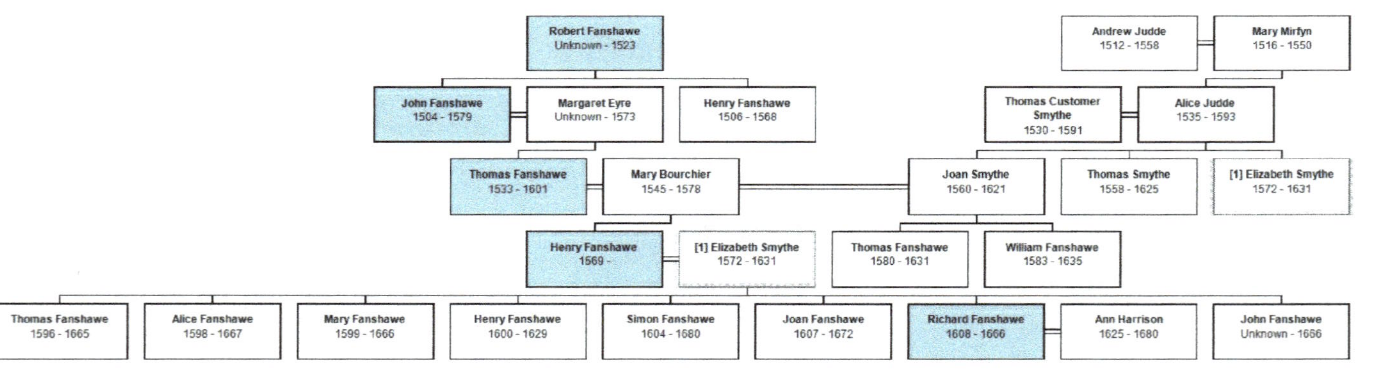

Introduction

The Fanshawe family originated in Derbyshire and gained wealth and status as holders of the office of King's (or Queen's) Remembrancer of the Exchequer. Their estates included Ware Park in Hertfordshire, and in Essex, Jenkins in Barking and Parsloes in Dagenham. They were staunchly loyal to King Charles I during the Civil War, and as a result their fortune was almost wiped out. However, the family's education, style, manners and connections were firmly established, and succeeding generations left their mark on history. Sir Richard Fanshawe (1608-66) represents the high point in the family aspirations.

Richard was the tenth child of Sir Henry Fanshawe of Ware Park, the third Fanshawe to hold the office of Remembrancer. Sir Henry was a prominent member of the cultured courts of Elizabeth I and James I. He remodelled the house and grounds at Ware Park in the fashionable Italian Renaissance style. Sir Henry was a noted patron of the arts and retained the composer John Ward in his household for many years. He kept a London house in Warwick Lane, near St. Paul's Cathedral.

Richard's mother, Elizabeth Smythe, was the youngest daughter of Thomas 'Customer' Smythe, who owned the rights to collect customs duties at the Port of London and was one of the wealthiest merchants and financiers of the time. One of Richard's uncles, Sir Thomas Smythe, was the first Governor of the Virginia Company and Ambassador to the court of the Czar of Russia.

Sir Henry Fanshawe died in 1616 when Richard was eight. Richard attended Thomas Farnaby's School in Cripplegate, then at the age of 15 entered Jesus College, Cambridge where he excelled at Greek and Latin. Obeying his mother's wish he entered the Inner Temple, though he had no great interest in the law and abandoned it after his mother's death in 1631.

Richard joined his Smythe cousins in Paris, staying there for a year. He then journeyed alone to Spain, made connections at the Spanish court and became fluent in the language. During this time he rediscovered his boyhood love of writing poetry and also made English translations of classical works.

In 1635 Richard was appointed Secretary to the British Embassy in Madrid, and in 1640 was promoted to Secretary for the Council of War in Ireland. The Civil War erupted two years later, and by 1643 Richard had joined the exiled court of Charles I at Oxford. Within a year he was appointed Secretary of War for the 14 year-old Prince of Wales.

On 18 May 1644 at Wolvercote Church, just outside Oxford, Richard married Ann Harrison, daughter of Sir John Harrison of Balls Park in Hertfordshire. Sir John had risen from a junior post in the Customs House to become a major City financier. Richard and Ann were distant cousins, her mother being Margaret Fanshawe. By a quirk of fate, Richard was also related to the Parliamentary leader Oliver Cromwell, both being descended from Thomas Mirfyn of Ely.

Ann Fanshawe's spirited, independent and passionate personality shines from her Memoirs. Through these and Richard's personal correspondence we have a unique insight into their lives, through the turbulent years of the Civil War, then after the Restoration in the court of Charles II and European diplomatic circles. Mutual strength and determination was the cornerstone of their marriage, as Ann writes:

> *...we never had but one mind throughout our lives, our souls were wrapped up in each other, our aims and designs one, our loves one, and our resentments one. We so studied the other's mind in our looks; whatever was real happiness, God gave it me in him.*

Charles I was executed on 30 January 1649 whilst Richard was in Ireland as Treasurer of War to the Fleet, but he immediately travelled to the young King Charles II in The Hague. He was commanded to return to Ireland to raise funds, and with his family he travelled extensively throughout Ireland, and then to Madrid to seek aid from the Spanish Court.

After the Battle of Worcester in September 1651, Richard was captured and imprisoned at Whitehall. Thanks to Ann's determination and strength of will, he was eventually released on bail of £4000, which weighed heavily on the family fortune. Richard was under virtual house arrest for several years, only permitted to travel within five miles of his home, Tankersley Park in Yorkshire. He used this period of forced inactivity to concentrate on writing, translating and publishing poetry. Later he was allowed to live at Homerton, Huntingdonshire, with his sister Alice, widow of Sir Capel Bedel.

Following the death of Oliver Cromwell in 1658, Richard and Ann fled to the Continent to join the exiled court of Charles II. At the Restoration of the monarchy in 1660 Richard travelled with the King back to England, and was awarded a baronetcy. Being fluent in Portuguese, he helped negotiate the King's marriage contract with Catherine of Braganza. He wrote personal letters to Catherine on behalf of Charles, then went to Portugal to complete the arrangements (and draft Catherine's replies, in English, to the King!)

In 1662 Sir Richard was appointed Ambassador to Portugal, and two years later became Ambassador to Spain. He was also a member of the Privy Council and the Order of the Garter.

As Ambassador, Sir Richard was charged by Lord Arlington, the Secretary of State, with negotiating a peace treaty between Spain and Portugal whilst securing beneficial trade agreements for English merchants. Sir Richard received agreement in principle from London for his draft treaty, but at that time communications were slow and insecure. After waiting months for a response, Sir Richard exercised his own judgement, based on the known facts, and signed a conditional treaty with Spain. He then left for Lisbon to try to secure Portugal's agreement.

On hearing that the Earl of Sandwich was on his way to Spain as Ambassador Extraordinary, Sir Richard returned to Madrid. He was shocked to learn that the Earl would be replacing him as Ambassador to Spain and he himself was to return to London. On 15 June 1666, before he could leave Madrid, Sir Richard fell ill with a severe fever and died on Saturday 26 June.

Lady Ann and her children made the gruelling journey back to England with Sir Richard's coffin, eventually landing at Tower Wharf, London in November 1666. The city had been devasted by the Great Fire just two months previously.

In her Memoirs, Ann defends her husband's reputation and honour. She is outraged at the unjust treatment he received. She is particularly aggrieved by the fact that he had been a faithful servant and loyal friend to Charles II for many years, but the King ignored her plea for help in bringing his body back to England. Ann dedicated the rest of her life to reclaiming Sir Richard's honourable name, reputation and wealth. She died in early 1680 and was buried on 20 January alongside her husband in the Fanshawe vault at St Mary's Church, Ware.

Children of Sir Richard and Lady Ann

Lady Ann records that she gave birth to 14 living children. In addition four babies were stillborn, including triplet boys. Only one son and three daughters survived to adulthood. Lady Ann was often pregnant while undertaking difficult and dangerous journeys across Europe. When her infant children died they were buried quickly and left in distant places.

The son, Richard, succeeded to the baronetcy, but he suffered an unspecified disability. He never married, and the title became extinct on his death in 1694.

Their surviving daughters

Margaret (1653 -1705) was born at Tankersley Park. She married Vincent Grantham of Goltho, and although she had two sons no male heirs followed. Ann was born in 1654 at Frogpool, the home of Sir Richard's sister Joan and her husband Sir Philip Warwick. Ann is said to have married a Mr Ryder, and

Charlotte Coleman, who first published Lady Ann's memoirs in 1829 in association with the Reverend Charles Robert Fanshawe, was acknowledged to be Ann Ryder's grand-daughter. Little is known about the third surviving daughter, Elizabeth (born 1662), beyond her marriage to Christopher Blount in 1684.

The author: H.C. Fanshawe

Herbert Charles Fanshawe (1852-1923) was born in Durham, the son of the Reverend John Faithfull Fanshawe and grandson of Charles Robert Fanshawe who had originally published Lady Ann's memoirs. He was educated at Repton School and entered the Indian Civil Service, rising to become Commissioner of the Delhi Division.

On retirement, H.C. Fanshawe researched and wrote two monumental works on his family. The first was his 1907 edition of the Memoirs of Ann Lady Fanshawe, which includes several appendices and almost 300 pages of notes. The other was the History of the Fanshawe Family (published in 1927) from which this extract on Sir Richard is taken. H.C. Fanshawe had died in March 1923 and the book was completed by his relative Beaujulois Mabel Ridout (nee Fanshawe). They had collaborated on the research preparation, travelling widely inspecting primary sources.

In many respects the History of the Fanshawe family is a sequel to the 1907 edition of Ann Fanshawe's Memoirs. H.C. Fanshawe intended them to be read in conjunction. As only a few copies of each were printed, their availability is now limited. As part of the Sir Richard Fanshawe 350 commemoration during 2016, Valence House Publications intends to issue facsimile editions of both works.

Valence House: the Fanshawe family research hub

Valence House in Dagenham was first recorded in a property deed of 1269, and the earliest surviving part dates from the 15th century. From the second half of the 16th century until the early 17th century it was owned by the

Fanshawe family. The only member of the family to actually live there was Susanna Fanshawe and her husband Timothy Lucy.

In 1963 Captain Aubrey Fanshawe of Bratton Fleming, Devon, donated 49 family portraits to Valence House. A further seven were given by the family in 2004. The collection has been augmented by works purchased through private sale and auctions. The original gift also included archives such as Sir Richard's diplomatic papers, and the library and research papers amassed by H. C. Fanshawe in the course of his research. Many volumes are annotated and indexed by him.

Valence House is home to Barking and Dagenham's local history museum and Archives and Local Studies Centre. It has been praised by Museums Journal as "one of the best local history museums in Greater London". For more information and opening times please see: www.valencehousecollections.co.uk

Further reading

Editions of Lady Ann Fanshawe's Memoirs are freely downloadable from Project Gutenberg or Google Books

Richard Fanshawe: Shorter poems and translations (edited by N.W. Bawcutt) 1964

Richard Fanshawe: The Lusiads (translation of the original by Luis de Camoes, edited by Geoffrey Bullough) 1963

Gareth Alban Davies: Sir Richard Fanshawe, Hispanist Cavalier (1977)

William Eugene Simone: Sir Richard Fanshawe: an account of his life and writings (1950)

Roger M Walker & W H Liddell: From Bilbao to Becontree – the previous history of Sir Richard Fanshawe, Bart., in Valence House Museum (1996)

Roger M Walker & W H Liddell: The papers of Sir Richard Fanshawe, Bart. (1999)

The Descendants of Sir Richard and Lady Fanshawe

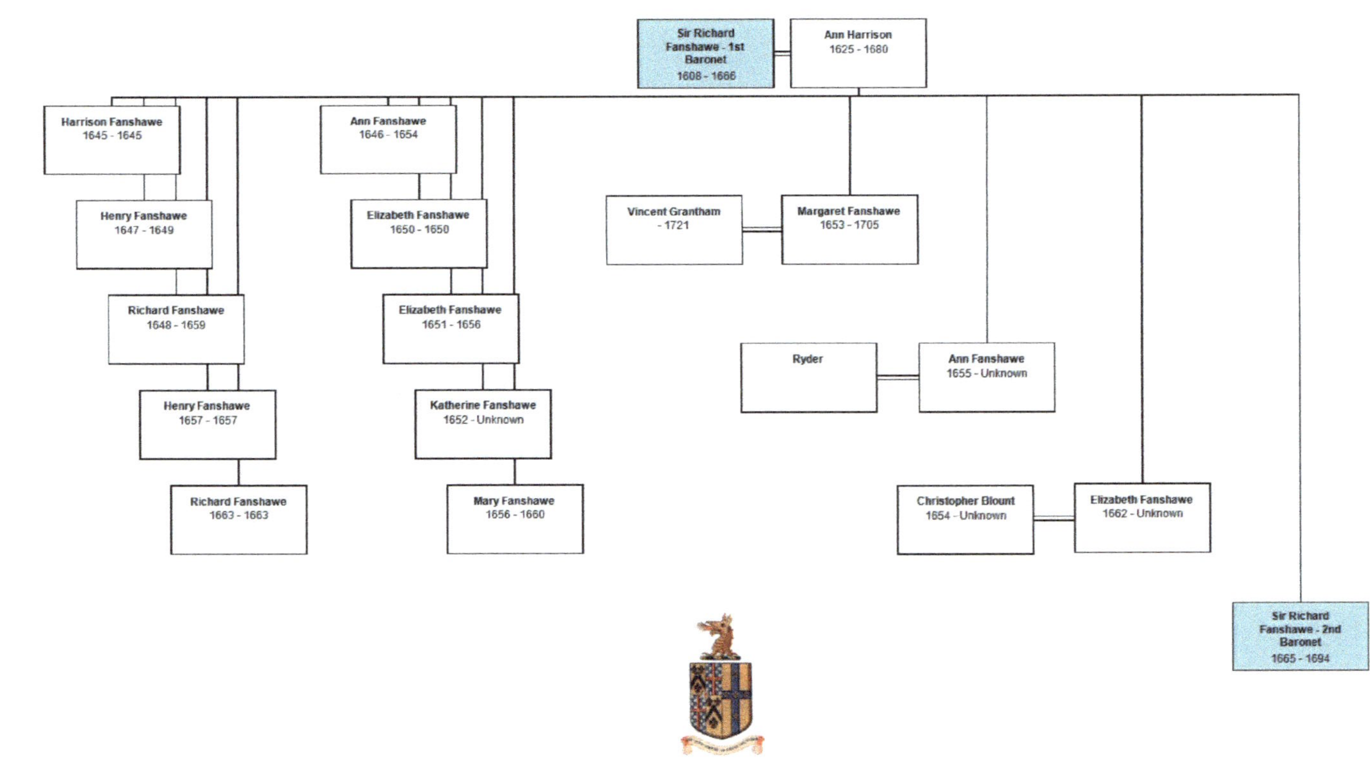

The Fanshawe crest

from The History of the Fanshawe Family (1927)

CHAPTER VI.

Sir Richard Fanshawe, Bart.

> "*As you are certainly a gentleman; thereto*
> *Clerk-like, experienc'd (which no less adorns*
> *Our gentry, than our parents' noble names,*
> *In whose success we are gentle*); "
>
> *Winter's Tale*, I., ii.

A good deal of information regarding Sir Richard Fanshawe has happily come to light since the annotated edition of his wife's *Memoirs* was published in 1907.

The beautiful old font at which he was christened on 15 June, 1608, still stands in the parish church of St. Mary, Ware: it is of the end of the XIV. century, and is decorated by carved scenes, in which the figures appear in the dress and armour of the date, representing the Annunciation (two scenes), St. Margaret and the dragon, St. Christopher and the child, St. George and the dragon, St. Katherine, St. James in pilgrim weeds, and St. John the Baptist. At the angles between the scenes are 8 angels with instruments of the Passion and of music. Of his boyhood naturally there is nothing more to record; but it may be noticed that among the pictures of Lord Bathurst is a charming one by Mytens of Lady Apsley and her son, the second Sir Allen (*Memoirs*, p. 362) born 1616, which no doubt closely represents the costume in which Richard Fanshawe and his mother would have appeared about 1615.

Besides other distinguished scholars at Dr. Farnaby's school, was Edward King, the Lycidas of Milton; Richard Fanshawe was probably a day boarder there, the family house in Warwick Lane lying only half a mile distant from Red Cross Street and Goldsmith's Alley.

In a manuscript volume* in the British Museum (*Addl. MSS.*, 15228) which contains several of the early published pieces of Sir Richard Fanshawe, and of which much is undoubtedly in his autograph writing, there are a number of translations from Boethius (nearly all the metrical portions) and Martial (13 epigrams), and some decidedly tasteful poems of personal application. From one of these headed "Splendidis longe valedico nugis" the following may be quoted:—

"Yee Vanity's of humane Race,
That lead fond youth the wild-goose chase,
Mindless of after good;
Bee gone, y'ore understood.
But thou my Darling Vanity,
ffoe to my thriving, Poetry,
Whose love, begunne at first,
My unwise Tutor nurst;
What witch with her inchanting rodd,
Can loose me from thy chains, what God?
Not Pegasus can mee
ffrom thy chymeras free.
. . . .
Younger brothers must not wedd
As they are by affection ledd;
Alas! if that might bee,
I'dd wive no art but thee.
As 'tis both parts it doth behove
To leave betimes this foolish love,
And enter wiser bands:
Then here lett us break hands.
Then catch some heire (there's none will shunne
To meet thee) I to the law will run;
Nor thou; unless tho'udst rather
Wee kept in hell together."

Another poem runs in part:—

"My quencht and discontented Muse
Her idle fyres again renewes;
Which from my course do mee withdraw,
The thrieving Law.
Whence the free councells of my friends,
Nor my own choyce of better ends,
Nor this poor pleading without fee
Can ransome me.

* It is hoped that this volume may be published some day with the printed works, or at least with a large selection from the printed works of Sir Richard Fanshawe.

Sir Richard Fanshawe as a young man

Engraving from a portrait by Sir Peter Lely

LBBD Archives at Valence House

The Oxford Arms

Near the Fanshawe family home in Warwick Lane close to St Paul's Cathedral

LBBD Archives at Valence House

I would not fain spin out my braynes
In Rhyme; This breast such work disdaynes,
And something that to worth aspires
ffaintly desires."

These are specially interesting as, knowing Richard Fanshawe's distaste for the law, "so crabbed a study and disagreable to his inclinations," as his wife records (*Memoirs*, p. 27)—an opinion which his cousin John Evelyn shared, terming it an "impolished study." Another graceful poem "On the sight of a gentlewoman in church" opens with the happy stanza:—

"Yett shee was fayre, yett did her grace
Her meaner beautyes much advance;
And I prefer'd before her face
Her countenance.

These poems and the translations were presumably written before he started on his travels in 1632, and two poems "On the report of fower Kings dead at once" and "Upon the newes of the King of Sweden's death" belong to the close of that year. The latter opens with the strong lines:—

"I'l not beleiv't, if fates could be so cross
Nature would not be silent of her loss."

A picture of the Earl of Bedford, with a dwarf page, painted by Printzer in 1627, must represent him much as he was when Richard Fanshawe went with him to Madrid in 1633. As noted in the Woburn Catalogue this Earl, who became the first Duke of Bedford, lived from the reign of James I. "through the civil war with its heroes on either side, the Restoration and its brilliant Court, and the downfall of James II.," to within two years of that of Queen Anne.

Some slight additional information regarding the years of his early residence in Madrid, 1635-38 (*Memoirs*, pp. 339-41), is to be found in the *Tixall Papers* (edited by Arthur Clifford, 1813). Howell reported at the end of July, 1635, that Lord Aston with whom he went to Spain, was about to take leave of the King, and on the 3 August the *Henrietta Maria* was ordered to be ready for the Ambassador at Portsmouth; but he did not sail till 23 September nor reach Madrid till about the middle of November.* As we know from the public records Fanshawe was back again in London in August, 1636; for a second time—after a very short stay at Madrid—in May, 1637, on which occasion Lord Aston wrote to Sir Francis Windebank of him as " a gentleman whom I finde I might safely employ in greater trusts "; and for a third time in January, 1638; returning to Madrid at the end of April.

In a letter from Lord Aston's daughter Constantia (afterwards married to W. Fowler) to her brother Herbert with her father, she refers to Mr. Fanshawe's visit to them on the first occasion and explains the circumstances in which he composed the following verses: " We had bin one evening at Bowles, and when we came in my sister (Gertrude Aston) was opening her hayre with her fingers and bade him tell you that she would not curle her hayre otherwise than it curled itselfe till she saw you againe." This is the last poem in the MSS. Volume of the British Museum, and the omission from that of the poem on the *Sovereign of the Seas* which is dated 1637 tends to show that the copying of the verses in it was finished in the former year:—

Cælia hath for a brother's absence sworne
(Rash oath) that since her tresses can not mourne
In blacke (because unshorne Apollo's hayre
Darts not a greater splendo^r through the Ayre;)
Shee'l make them droope in her neglect; forgett
Those rings which her white hand in order sett,
And curiously did ev'ry morning curle
Into a thousand snares the wanton purle.
Butt they are disobedient to command;
And sweare they owe no homage to her hand;

* Lord Aston was married to the daughter of Sir John Sadleir of Standon, Herts., and was no doubt well acquainted with Sir Henry Fanshawe; and on this account presumably, Richard Fanshawe was attached to his staff. His town residence was at the Mulberry Garden, now included in the grounds of Buckingham Palace. His son was, like himself, a Roman Catholic and therefore much in the shade from 1638-60.

That nature is their mistress, in her name
The priviledge that they were borne to claime,
Skorning to have it said the hayre gave place
To the perfections that all parts doe grace;
So weave themselves in wreaths and curle now more
My carelessness than by her care before.
Like a crispt comet which the stars pursue
In thronges and mortalls with pale horror view
Threatning some great ones death, such light displays
Her brow, or like a Saint thats Crown'd with Rayes
Lady, what bootes neglect of face or hayre
You must use art if you will grow less fayre."

On the two subsequent visits to England the Secretary was not able to spare time to visit Lord Aston's home at Tixall. On the latter of these the same daughter wrote " Mr. Fanshawe has made us believe a great while he would come downe, but it seems his business is such it will not permit him; for he has just this day sent us letters of yours, which he has kept all this time thinking to bring them himselfe . . . Mr. Fanshaw sent me word he went within two days." A note of his life, among the *Tixall papers*, states that Lord Aston was so badly paid in Spain that he had to raise £30,000 to clear off his debts, and so parted with much property, and Sir Richard Fanshawe recorded 25 years later that Lord Aston had not increased his estate by accepting this employment, and that Sir Arthur Hopton, who no doubt received nothing from Charles I. for many years, had reduced his from £6000 to £1000 *p.a.*

In September, 1638, the Secretary received a payment of £500 for his ordinary and extraordinary charges whilst he was employed " upon his Ma[ties] service into Spaine." An item of special interest is one from a letter of Archbishop Laud of 14 June, 1637, to Lord Aston, in which the former writes to " His Ma[ties] Embassador in the Courte of Spayne at Madrid," " I have received your Lordship's letters by your Secretary," to wit Richard Fanshawe, who was thus known at least to the Archbishop as well as to the Earl of Strafford, whom he served as Secretary to the Council for War (*Memoirs*, p. 343) on a pay of 25s per diem.

His election as M.P. for Ballinakill, one of the rotten boroughs created by King James I. for the purpose of controlling the Irish Parliament, must have been after 18 March, 1640, when the vacancy was ordered to be filled, and he could not therefore have been of the House when it voted four subsidies of £180,000 on 23 March, at the orders of the Viceroy. The correspondence quoted on p. 344 of the *Memoirs*, shows that Richard Fanshawe was still in Ireland when the Earl of Strafford was executed on 8 May, 1641.

Two months after his return from there, Richard Fanshawe was appointed King's Remembrancer in place of his eldest brother, on 5 August, 1641; and seems to have lived in Warwick Lane, as he dates a letter to Sir P. Perceval from there on 18 March, 1642: orders to him as Remembrancer are on record up to December of that year.* In the spring following, according to Lady Fanshawe, he went to Oxford; and apparently he was there before she joined her father at a baker's in a back street, as the Stoke Rochford papers indicate that Sir John Harrison proceeded to Oxford some time in August, 1643. The *Cambridge Modern History* (Vol. IV., 454) records that "many officials of the Exchequer had followed the King to Oxford carrying with them that mysterious knowledge which was necessary for the working of that ancient institution." Of the gathering of Ladies at Oxford, Clarendon notes, truly no doubt if not very gallantly, that they and the court and nobility and gentry "bore any kinds of alarm very ill," the place not being tolerably fortified nor the garrison well provided. The statement of Lady

* Among the Clerks of the King's Remembrancer, recorded in January, 1641-2, with the Remembrancer Richard Fanshawe, were Anthony Bourchier the younger, Sir Simon Fanshawe, and Ellis Young. Among those of Sir Peter Osborne were his sons Henry and John, and William Wymondsall. George Long was Master of the Office of Pleas so he and Sir Richard must have been acquainted before they met on the Council of the Prince of Wales in 1645.

Sir Richard Fanshawe (1608-1666)

by William Dobson (1644)

Valence House Museum

Ann Fanshawe (1625-80), wife of Sir Richard Fanshawe

by Cornelius Johnson

Valence House Museum

Fanshawe that her husband was made Secretary of War to the Prince of Wales when he had been about a year in Oxford, and shortly before her marriage on 18 May, 1644, is confirmed by a letter of Thomas Windebank of 25 May, in which he complains of being passed over for Fanshawe's office, which, however, he designates as the Secretaryship of the Council of the Prince; and later Lady Fanshawe refers to this appointment as "secrettary of ye Councell of war" to the Prince.

Fanshawe's translation of the Pastor Fido might run:—

> "in this jolly month of May
> when earth is clad in all her best array."

but the marriage took place in the May of 1644 in the midst of circumstances of war. On the very day of it the King returned to Oxford from "slighting" Reading. A week later the royalist garrison at Abingdon was withdrawn, and the next day the Parliament's cavalry swept round the south-west side of the city and occupied Cowley and Shotover; and on the 3 June the King proceeded north to face Sir William Waller. Curiously enough the Secretary at War did not accompany his master when the latter went with the King into the west in the summer of 1644, and was present at the second battle of Newbury at the end of October, his wife recording that he parted with her for the first time in March, 1645: no doubt his recent marriage held him excused when the Prince joined his father during the brief campaign of muddled marches, which ended in the battle of Cropredy Bridge and the death of Sir William Boteler on 29 June, 1644.

Their eldest son, Harrison, was born at Trinity College on 23 February, 1645, and Sir Edward Hyde's son Edward, who died in January, 1665, was baptized at All Souls' College on 1 April following. The former was buried in the chapel of Merton College, then the parish church of St. John's, and the latter in Westminster Abbey, where his father and mother also lie, at the foot of the steps to the chapel of King Henry VII.

The Prince of Wales was declared General in the West on 26 January, 1645; and on the following day Richard Fanshawe must have discharged one of his earliest duties as Secretary for War to the Prince's Council, when he signed the commission appointing Lord Capel to be Captain General of His Highness' Guard, which that nobleman not only raised but also paid.

There was a special reason why Sir William Parkhurst* should deliver to Lady Fanshawe the first money which her husband sent to Oxford after leaving her in March, 1645, as he was Master of the Mint there: a medal bearing his effigy by Thomas Rawlings had been struck at Oxford in the previous year. There was also a special reason why Sir Marmaduke Rawdon should offer his escort to Lady Fanshawe when she left Oxford to go to Bristol, as it was less than a month since Cromwell, after capturing Blechenden house on 24 April, had attempted "by sheer force of audacity to drive Faringdon Castle to surrender. The commander of the castle kept his head cool, and Cromwell not having the means to hand to suit the action to the word, was compelled to leave the achievement unaccomplished" (*Gardner, Civil War*); and *Diurnals* of early May report two attacks from Faringdon on the forces of Colonels Cromwell and Whalley.† Of the ravage of plague in Bristol in the early summer of 1645 it is recorded that

* Sir William Parkhurst, knighted 1619, was Master of the Mint under James I., as well as under Charles I. and II. He was buried in the Tower Church in March, 1667, and must no doubt have been an old man then. The well known royalist money with the motto Exsurgat (Deus dissipentur inimici) was issued by him from the Oxford Mint, and his receipts for plate contributed to the Mint by various colleges and private persons, still exist.

† Sir Marmaduke Rawdon married Elizabeth Thorowgood (heiress of an old Hoddesdon family), who was buried at Hoddesdon in 1667. Dugdale records his death at Faringdon as on 26 April, 1646, the day before the King left Oxford for the last time. The picturesque Jacobean house which he built there in 1622 still faces all passers along the great northern road, as it faced Lady Fanshawe whenever she journeyed from London to Balls Park.

3000 deaths took place; and Barnstaple, to which the Prince of Wales and the Fanshawes removed from Bristol, paid a death toll of 1500.* Nothing fresh has come to light regarding their sojourn in the West. Of the three ladies who dabbled in the "knowledge of state affairs" (*Memoirs*, p. 34) no one lived till the Restoration. Richard Fanshawe was much too versed in Spanish caution:—

Tu secreto en qualquier cosa
 Communicate contigo,
 Y no obligues a tu amigo
A carga tan peligrosa.

to be snared by the attempt to get information out of him. The statement in the notes to the *Memoirs* (p. 356) that a portrait of Lady Rivers represents her in late Elizabethan dress, is a mistake, this being a picture of Mary Countess Rivers, her mother. A likeness by Lely of the daughter Elizabeth, Countess Rivers in her own right, exists however, and is reproduced in Farrer's "*Portraits in West Sussex Houses*." She wears a low cut black dress with four ropes of pearls across the front, and has dark bushy hair curled on both sides of her head, and a jewelled comb across it at the back. Two pictures of Lady Isabella Thynne once existed: the first, by Vandyk, is still at Longleat and represents her in a white dress with a green scarf streaming behind her as she moves rapidly to the right carrying in her left hand, in front of her, a large lute, probably the very one of which Waller wrote:—

"The trembling strings about her fingers crowd,
And tell their joy for ev'ry kiss aloud:
Small force there needs to make them tremble so;
Touch'd by that hand, who would not tremble too?"

The other was a picture by Lely, no doubt the one which

* Sir William Apsley, the Governor of Barnstaple, was connected with the Fanshawes; his mother, and the wife of Sir George Ayliffe, of Grittenham, Wilts. (whose son John Ayliffe married Katherine Fanshawe in 1636—*Memoirs*, p. 291), being sisters, and daughters of Sir John St. John of Lydiard Tregoze. One of Sir George's daughters was named Apsley.

Evelyn saw on 15 February, 1649, and of which Charles Cotton wrote the happy verses:—

Nature and art are here at strife,
The shadow comes so near the life;
Sit still (dear Lely) thou'st done that
Thyself must love and wonder at.
. . . . . . Surely she sat
Thy pencil thus to celebrate
Above all others that could claim
An echo from the voice of fame . .
. . . . . . But thou canst go
No further than what art can do;
And when all's done, this thou hast made
Is but a robber kind of shade;
And thou though thou hast played thy part,
A painter, no creator, art.

Lady Isabella, who was born on 6 October, 1623, was buried at Kensington church on 10 April, 1657, sixteen months before her sister Lady Diana; the entry of her burial being:—

"The Layday Esabella Thin from Queen St."

The gossiping Aubrey records that each of these sisters encountered an apparition of herself in the gardens of the present Holland House before she died.

The third of the trio, Lady Aubigny, was celebrated by lines addressed to her by Ben Jonson:—

"Only thus much out of a ravished zeal
Unto your name and goodness of your life
They speak; since you are truly that rare wife
Other great wives may blush at, when they see
What your tried manners are, what theirs should be."

While the Prince was in Exeter the unlucky Herrick wrote of him:—

What fate decreed, Time now has made us see
A renovation of the West by thee

. . . .

Something there yet remains for thee to do,
Then reach those ends that thou wast destined to.

. . . .

Meanwhile the prophets watch by watch shall pray,
While Young Charles fights and fighting wins the day."

Fuller recorded more truthfully and wittily that after the defeat of Langport which was rather a flight than a fight, "henceforward the sun of the King's cause declined, verging more and more westward till at last it set in Cornwall and since (after a long and dark night) rose again by God's goodness in the east when our gracious sovereign arrived at Dover."

Not less unfortunate were Herrick's lines addressed to Lord Hopton ("whom" wrote General Fairfax, "for personal worth and many virtues we honour and esteem above any of your party," and whom Sir Edward Hyde described "as faultless a person, as full of courage industry integrity and religion as I ever new man"):—

"Go on brave Hopton to effectuate that
Which we and times to come shall wonder at;
Lift up thy sword, next suffer it to fall,
And by that one blow set an end to all."

These anticipations were as unfortunate as Sir Richard's own, addressed to Charles II., as Prince of Wales, in 1646, upon the character of a Good King:—

"And he again with this more tender grown,
More Father of his People, on his own
Shoulders assumes their burthens, beats the way
Which they must tread, and is the first to obey
What he commands; to pardon others prone,
Inexorable to himself alone.
Neither in Diet, Cloathes, or Train will He
Exceed those banks should bound 'een Majesty;
Nor rush like beasts to Venus, but confine
His chaste desires to his own genial Vine."

According to the defence of his conduct which Sir Robert Long made in January, 1652, the Prince spent the Christmas of 1645 at Dartmouth, going there from Truro, and left soon after on the beating up of Chudleigh, Dartmouth being taken some days later. (It was surrendered on 18 January, 1646.) Long added "In all that business of the west I was not of the councell nor made any despatches of any publique business whatsoever, neyther was I trusted with the custody of any letters nor privy to any of his then Majesties affairs managed by the Prince and councell, for all of which Mr. Fanshaw was Secretary and wholely trusted " (*Clarendon State Papers, Bodleian* 42, p. 304).

By a double slip Lady Fanshawe states in her *Memoirs* that the pass given to Lady Capel and her daughter was granted by the Earl of Essex, and that Mr. Long was suspected of private intelligence with that General; but he had been relieved of his command, and had been succeeded on 21 January, 1645, by Sir Thomas Fairfax, who gave the King his fatal defeat at Naseby on 14 June. *The Perfect Diurnal* of 25-28 October states that Lady Capel obtained her pass in that month when the siege of Exeter was about to be commenced, and that Lady Hopton and Mistress Ashburnham also left the Royalist forces then.

The only other point of interest during the stay in the west is the record of the second marriage of Sir John Harrison at Madron Church in January, 1646.*

Admiral Batten had been ordered in December, 1645, to prevent the Prince's transportation to Falmouth; and the retreat to the Scilly Islands was a hopeless move, as without ships to maintain communications it could have been a question of weeks only before the Royalists were driven to surrender by starvation.

* It occurred to the editor of this family History, from consideration of the facts which Lady Fanshawe records in the *Memoirs*—that early in 1646 she was at Penzance with her father and her brother Fanshawe and his family, out of which her father had then married his new wife—and that the burial of a daughter of Sir Thomas Fanshawe took place at Madron (then the Parish church of Penzance) on 10 December, 1645, that this marriage might also have taken place at Madron; and on reference to the registers of that church, it was found that they contained an entry which indubitably records the fact. It occurs in the month of January, 1646, and though it is practically illegible now it was read 50 years ago, when Mr. Pridmore made the transcript from which the contents of the registers were published by Mr. G. B. Millet in 1877 (a fact unknown at the time to the Editor). Mr. Pridmore's copy runs " Sir John Harcis levinge in the borough of Swansea and Marye . . . daughter of . . . . within the Pishe of Maddorne." The transcriber could have had no knowledge of the persons to whom the entry related, and no reasonable individual can challenge the belief that the marriage recorded was that of Sir John Harrison then residing at Penzance (which might easily be misread for Swansea) and Mary Shotbolt his second wife.

Clarendon notes that during the Prince's whole stay, victuals for 2 days had not come out of Cornwall,* and nothing had come from France, so that the Prince's escape to Jersey was nearly as great a miracle as that after Worcester. Sir Edward Hyde's description of the position at Scilly, in a letter to the Marquis of Ormonde of 8 March, 1645, fully confirms Lady Fanshawe's account: "a place very strong of itself, and capable of being easily made impregnable" (with sufficient fleet, guns, and soldiers); "but as full of present wants and disacommodations as can be imagined." From *Chevalier's Record* of the stay of the Prince of Wales in Jersey it appears that Sir Richard accompanied him to the main land at Coutainville on 23 June, and then returned to the Island. The first mention of him by the Jersey annalist in his quaint island patois,† refers under the date of 19 April, 1646, to the arrival among other gentlemen of the Prince's suite, of "monsieur fincbess segretaire du prince le quel a menit (amenait) sa fāme avec luy en Jersey aux quels dieu donnet un enfant en Jersey, il a menit aussy la sœur de sa fāme a vecq sa fāme brave jeune demoiselle estant a la fleur de son age, les quels san (s'en) retournerent tous trois en semble en angleterre a londres durant les troubles et firent leurs paix." About 10-12 September, 1646, Chevalier notes their departure from Jersey, and that the ladies proceeded to London. Finally on 23 February, 1647, on their return to reclaim their baby girl, Chevalier gives a still fuller account of their movements recording: "lannuy (l'ennui) les prenont en jersey ils sanallerent a Can (Caen), et lessrent leurs anfant a nourice en jersey les deux fāmes de france sanallerent en angleterre a londres ou c'est q estoit leurs principal

* *Borlase* in 1753 notes that provisions from the mainland did not come to the Scilly Islands once in 17 weeks. The Duke Cosmo de Medici landed at St. Mary's in 1669, his pilot having originally mistaken Kinsale for the Cornish Port!

† *De Falle* notes of this that it "is not so properly a corrupt as an obsolete and antiquated French. For excepting the viciousness of pronuntiation it seems to be the very same as obtained in France in the reigns of Francis I. and Henry II."

bien, et monsieur finchess san allit trouver le prince a paris,* cependant q les fāmes estois a londre appetindrent p (or) faveur de faire revenir monsieur finchess a londres et eurent un passeport pour le faire revenir avecq elles a londre, et les fāmes rentrerent p (or) faveur en leurs moyans, car ils estois de grande maison et allier de grands parans a londre." "Sur le ranvoy des fāmes de londre a paris a mestre finchess il s'achemina vers londre pour aller trouver sa fāme q'y estoit, ou il fut bien recu des sieans, et aux reste ne fut troubler de personne autre. Estant a londres paissible sans qu'on leurs dit rien, ils s'y tindrent unne passe. Se voyant en repos en angleterre il se desliberer-ent de venir en Jersey luy et sa feme pour querir leurs anfant qui y estoit, et payer par les frets et charges du dit anfant, et aussy ils avoyant léssey (laissé) quelque hordes en Jersey qu'ils ranporterent. Les quels ne tarderent en Jersey q sept jours, puis san (s'en) retournerent par la voyee de france pour prendre passage de la pour angleterre. Sa fāme fut ranposeder de son bien pour les vivres; quand est pour le siean (sien) il ne le demanda point, se contentant q on le lessit (laissait) vivre en paix; car le parlement sestoit anparey (emparé) du revenut et des biens de ceux q avoyent embrace le partit du roy, et des fuygitifs y sanestois fuyis hors dangleterre. Estant an angleterre onne fit point de recherche appres luy, onne le lessit en paix," which shows that the Chevalier made good use of the seven days' stay of Richard Fanshawe and his wife in Jersey, to gain information about all their proceedings. Since they left the Island in February, 1647, Lady Fanshawe altogether confuses the occasion on which she recovered her island-born daughter, describing it to be after October in that year (*Memoirs*, p. 47).

The details of Richard Fanshawe's composition at

* The fact that Richard Fanshawe went to Paris to see his Master before returning to England, is confirmed by a letter of Sir Edward Hyde to Sir Thomas Darrel, referring to one of his of 31 October, 1646, and to the fact that "Dick Fanshawe met with you at his being in Paris."

the Goldsmiths Hall are given at p. 371 of the *Memoirs*. The value of the mediation of ladies in the business of compounding is specially recorded in the *Verney Memoirs* by Dr. Denton.* It is rather surprising to find that Fanshawe was allowed to go abroad in July, 1647, and again in October, and was not prevented from joining the Prince of Wales' fleet in the summer of the following year.

His first visit to the King was at Oatlands in the first half of August, for he left Jersey on 30 July, as we know from Chevalier, bearing a letter of the 27th from Hyde to the King and another from Lord Hopton; and an answer to the latter was sent by the emissary on 12 August from Oatlands, and a royal reply to the former was dated 19 August and was acknowledged by Hyde on 15 September (Lister's *Life of Clarendon*, III., 53, and *Clarendon State Papers*, Vol. II). The King went to Hampton Court on 24 August, 1647: we know exactly what the appearance of Charles I. was when Richard Fanshawe and his wife saw him there in August and September that year, for that is the very time when Lely painted the picture of him with the Duke of York, which is now in Sion House, and of which Lovelace wrote:—

"See what a clouded Majesty! and eyes
Whose glory through their mist doth brighter rise,
See! what a humble bravery doth shine,
And Griefs triumphant breaking thro' each line
Thou sorrow can'st design without a tear,
And with the man, his Beauty, Hope, or Feare."

* "Women were never so useful as now . . . I am confident if you were here you would do as our sages do, Instruct your wife and leave her to act it with the Committee. Their sex entitles them to many privileges and we find the comfort of them more now than ever." And a popular song on the subject ran:—

"The gentry are sequestered all;
Our wives you find at Goldsmiths' Hall,
For there they meet the Devil and all,
Still God a mercy Parliament."

The connection with Colonel Christopher Copley, through whose mediation Richard Fanshawe's compounding was effected, was that Copley's wife was a sister of Thomas Bosville of Warmsworth, who married Isabella Bullock, daughter of John Bullock of Norton and his wife Katherine Fanshawe, see p. 32.

Lely's picture of Ashburnham—whose blundering, together with that of Sir John Berkeley, brought to naught the attempt of the King to escape from Hampton Court—was no doubt painted by Lely at the same time. The Marquis of Ormonde came to England on 2 August, and was present at a Council held by the King at Hampton Court on 7 October; and it is probable that Richard Fanshawe met him again there. The luckless Herrick was more than ever unfortunate in his lines addressed to the King on his return to Hampton Court:—

"Enter and prosper while our eyes do wait
For an ascendant throu'ghly auspicate,
Under which sign we may the corner stone
Lay of our safety's new foundation.
That done O Cæsar live and be to us
Our fate, our fortune and our genius."

It seems impossible that Lady Fanshawe and her husband should have kissed the Queen's hand on Christmas Day, 1648, as stated on p. 49 of the *Memoirs*,* as she accompanied him as far as Calais† on his way to the Prince of Wales in Holland, and thence he was sent to Ireland, arriving in the latter country about 25 November, as is proved by a letter of the Marquis of Ormonde of 24 November, saying he was still expected; and another of the 27th, saying he had arrived. It had been proposed to send him there in the summer of

* Another slip on the preceding page of the *Memoirs* is that she welcomed the Marquesse of Ormonde from France in the summer of 1648. The Marquesse was parting with her husband at Caen about that time, and remained on there till August, 1652. The meeting must either refer to the latter year, or possibly it may be a reference to 1647, when the Marquesse followed her husband "out of *Ireland*."

† The fair traveller must often have seen the gate represented in Hogarth's picture of Calais. The dangerous condition of the roads leading from that port must have been of many years duration, as Sir Richard Verney makes special record of it in 1646, and Evelyn, in 1649 and 1650. The legend of the Barnacle goose, told by Sir Kenelm Digby at Calais, was one in common currency in the Channel Islands (Falle's *Cæsarea*)—Isaac Walton refers to the belief as held by Du Bartas, Camden, and Gerard the Herbalist, and Bishop Hall alludes to it mockingly in one of his Satires. Sir Kenelm Digby perhaps derived his information from a wonderful tractate published by Michael Maier at Frankfort in 1619. Before the *Memoirs* were written in 1676 Ray had declared the story to be an utter myth.

1646, and George Lord Digby then urged the Chancellor (of the Exchequer) if ever he had any influence with him, to come with Dick Fanshaw to Ireland; the Prince had specially recommended him to Ormonde on 23 June in that year (*Memoirs*, p. 370); and a fortnight after his return from sea the Prince wrote to Ormonde, " I intend immediately to send to you a gentleman with full instructions concerning all the particulars of yr. letter of 31 Aug[t]," and Hyde, writing to the same on the 13 October, 1648 (*Ormond Letters*, II., 358), said, " When I last troubled your Lordship I presumed to promise you a larger trouble by Mr. Fanshaw, who with great alacrity embraced the opportunity of serving the Prince that he might have the honour to wait on your Lordship; which happiness I so much envy him that I wish I might be a sharer with him by accompanying him to you. But since that fortune is yet too great for me I am glad he enjoys it who knows so much of my devotion to your lordship, and who (I presume) has worthily so much credit with your lordship as to be believed."

A day after his landing in Cork, Fanshawe delivered a message to Lord Inchiquin which the latter published in a long and interesting broad-sheet, of which a copy is in the Cambridge University Library. This was to the effect that a large fleet, victualled for three months and paid for six, was being at once sent to Ireland, with which the Duke of York would certainly come, and probably the Prince himself, when fully recovered from his illness at the Hague; that " the affections of his majesties people of England are in view of all the world more deeply rooted in them towards his majesty at this very time than ever "; that even if the Treaty of the Isle of Wight should not succeed, the Independent Army, whose success (won largely by using the King's name) the Irish Army might well follow, was likely to fall from its present position. " Why may not your time come . . . His Highness is verily persuaded in his mind that you are the men in whose power it is to pull that Independent party from the height of their designs . . . under a rough expostulation with them, according to their own way with the Parliament, your swords in your hands . . . what glory it will then be for this Army and country if the Prince of Munster, as they may call him, shall recover from hence by your valour and fidelity the Crown of England . . . or if you should but stand here mere spectators for a few months of the issue of things in England . . . His Highness thinks that this alone would go near to produce the same effect, and that you will soon be courted . . . in an open and honourable way by the best and also by the proudest of these. . . . This (I say) provided there be that firm unity and harmony among yourselves which is recommended." In conclusion the Envoy added, "Some of these particulars were not fully ripe as yet for public knowledge, I having had commission to speak them only to my Lord Lieutenant and your Lordship; but herein I obey your Lordship's command, not doubting of my master's approbation thereof, the rather because it is suitable to that gracious disposition which I have always observed in his Highness that the prevalent party in England (which thinks to roule (sic) the world before them for ever) should be warned, as well as his friends encouraged thereby. . . . But that two hopeful and inured Princes, a strong and resolved fleet, several well placed and fortified islands, and a faithful and courageous army (I sum up only what is in the hand, His Highness reckoning much more upon what is in the bush . . . for truth is great and will prevail) that these will I say be perpetually upon" [the] "skirts" [of the enemy] "and will be as so many continual goads in their sides, till they come to honourable conditions with his Majesty."

Unhappily none of these brave and encouraging words were to be fulfilled, as indeed, none of the personal promises of the Prince were; though Cliffe asserts, in his *History of the Irish Rebellion*, 1647, that they puffed up Lord Inchiquin and diverted him and Colonel

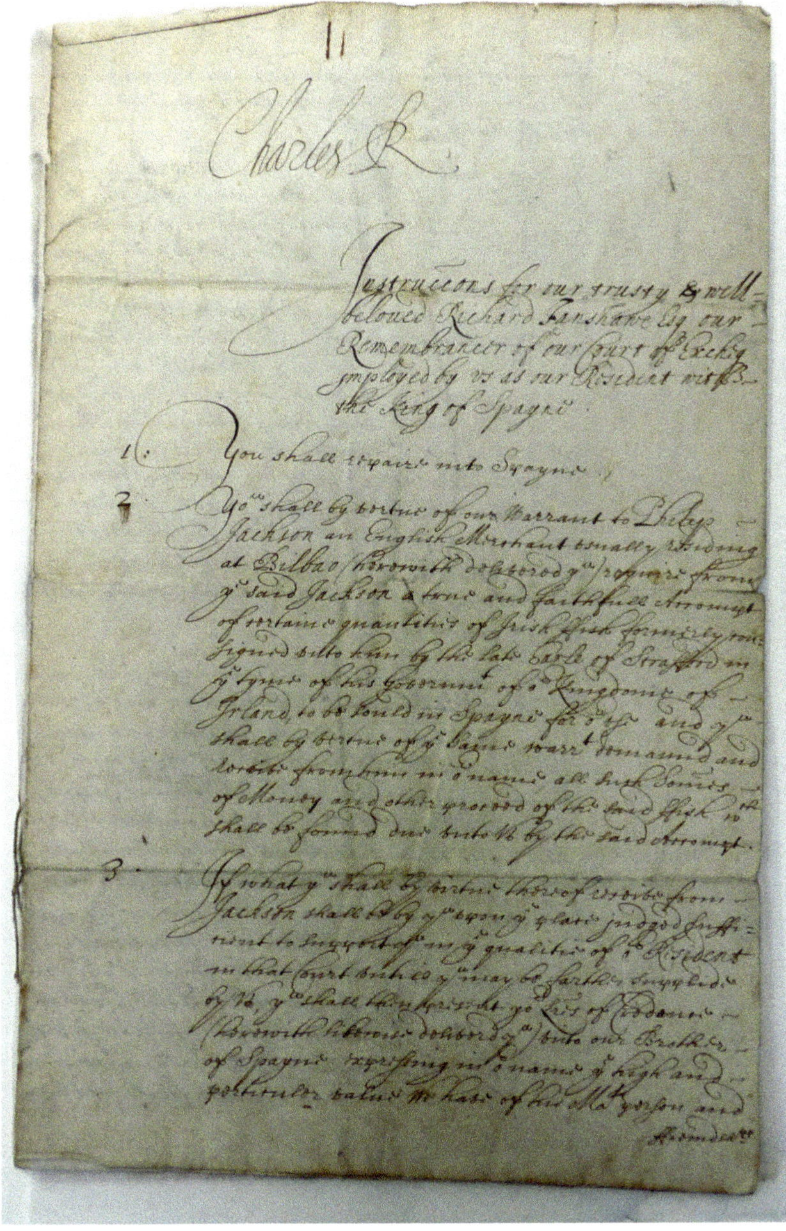
11

Charles R

Instructions for our trusty & well-beloved Richard Fanshawe Esq our Remembrancer of our Court of Excheq employed by us as our Resident with the King of Spayne.

1. You shall repaire unto Spayne.

2. You shall by vertue of our Warrant to Phillip Jackson an English Merchant usually residing at Bilbao (herewith delivered you) require from ye said Jackson a true and faithfull Accompt of certaine quantities of Irish fish formerly consigned unto him by the late Earle of Strafford in ye tyme of his Governmt of ye Kingdome of Ireland to be sould in Spayne for our use and you shall by vertue of ye same warrt demand and receive from him in our name all such Sumes of Money and other proceed of the said fish wch shall be found due unto Us by the said Accompt.

3. If what you shall by vertue thereof receive from Jackson shall be by you upon ye place judged sufficient to support you in ye qualitie of our Resident in that Court untill you may be farther supplyed by Us, you shall then present our Lres of Credence (herewith likewise delivered you) unto our Brother of Spayne expressing in our name ye high and particular value We have of his Mats person and

ffriendsh

Charles I to Richard Fanshawe instructions as Resident in Spain (signed by the King at the top)

19 October 1647 - Hampton Court

LBBD Archives at Valence House

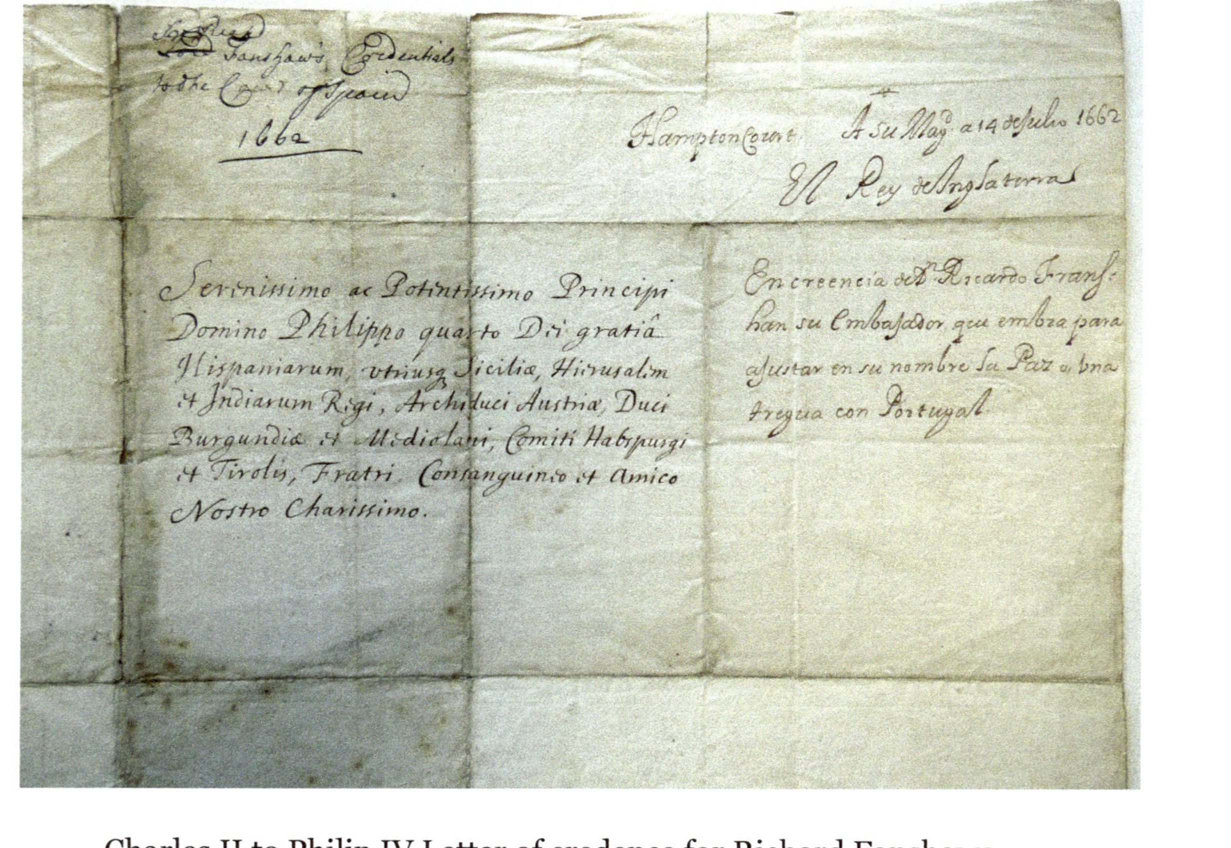
Sir Rich.d Fanshaw's Credentials
to the Court of Spain
1662

Hampton Court. A su Mag.d a 14 de Julio 1662
El Rey de Inglaterra

Serenissimo ac Potentissimo Principi
Domino Philippo quarto Dei gratiâ
Hispaniarum, utriusq Siciliæ, Hierusalem
et Indiarum Regi, Archiduci Austriæ, Duci
Burgundiæ et Mediolani, Comiti Habspurgi
et Tirolis, Fratri, Consanguineo et Amico
Nostro Charissimo.

En creencia de D. Ricardo Franshan su Embaxador que embia para
ajustar en su nombre la Paz o una
tregua con Portugal

Charles II to Philip IV Letter of credence for Richard Fanshawe
(Signature of Charles II on the back)

24 July 1662 - Hampton Court

LBBD Archives at Valence House

Townshend and others from continuing their overtures to the Parliament, which had been opened before the King's emissary arrived. If anything could be worse than the disunion and faction which prevailed in the west of England in 1645, it was the disunion and faction on all sides in Ireland with which the Marquis of Ormonde had to deal during the years 1648-50; and neither his devoted loyalty nor his courage were able to prevail against these fatal defects. In a long letter which he wrote to Sir Robert Long from Kilcolgan (from where the Marquis of Ormonde was himself to sail 10 months later) on 23 January, 1650, two weeks before leaving Ireland, Sir Richard summed up the then situation, by saying that though the Lord Lieutenant had succeeded in relieving Waterford, at much risk both from treachery and from the fact that his troops were as unwilling to garrison the town against Cromwell as the townsmen were to receive them, he had thereupon found his other troops dispersed to quarters without orders, which made it impossible for him to attempt anything against the weather-beaten and scattered English troops, who indeed were so pitifully battered it was said, that Cromwell did not stick to confess it that without the Revolters (of Cork and Youghal, etc.) he had been absolutely ruined before this time—a sad misreading of actual facts.

Since writing his last letter, Fanshawe had removed from Limerick to the midst of Thomond in County Clare; had then visited the Lord Lieutenant and accompanied him to the Earl of Clanricarde at Portumna, returning to Thomond where he found Lord Inchiquin, who had been in Kerry seeking to make places there secure the more so because of his "apprehensions of the great animosity conceived against him by the Irish."

On 7 February, 1650, a letter of Peters' reported: "The Lord Inchiquin is in Kerry in a great discontent and forlorn posture, not only refused by the Lord-Lieut. Cromwell but cast off by Ormond and by the popish Irish also, and at present under a cloud." And the next month it was recorded on 22 March: " Saturday was a fortnight Lord Broghill and Col. Hy. Cromwell fell on the L. Inchiquin's quarters near Limerick . . . The L. Inchiquin fled, narrowly escaping." The summary of the Lord Lieutenant's* position, which Fanshawe had written to Sir R. Long in a previous letter, is unfortunately not forthcoming.

It will be remembered that Lady Fanshawe joined her husband in Ireland in May, 1649; and as she had proceeded to England in the previous October or November, she must have been there—and possibly in London—at the time of the execution of the King. This is confirmed by a letter from Phineas Andrews to Sir John Harrison of the date of January, 1649 (*Stowe MSS.*, 184, f. 123), in which the former writes, " Your daughter ffanshawe has sent to her husband for sanction to deliver those writings which they challenge, and to that purpose they desire you will deal personally with them." From the Stoke Rochford papers it appears that the lands given to her in dowry which she sold " to him that is now Judge Archer," for £4000, early in this year, were situated in Theydon Garnon, Essex, and that the purchaser used pressure with Sir John Harrison to induce him to sell another farm in Epping which Sir John had reserved for himself.†

* Lord Morley, in his *Oliver Cromwell*, designates the Marquis of Ormonde as " one of the most admirably steadfast, patient, clear-sighted, and honorable 'men' in the list of British Statesmen " and every one who has studied the original papers of 1640-1680 can add a whole-hearted endorsement to this. Among the *Ormonde letters* published by Carte, is one from a Roman Catholic to a nobleman of the Court of Brussels of the date of February 1656 (*Carte*, Vol. II., p. 99), in which the former writes of the Marquis " of all the great men living I do believe him to be the most full of honour, integrity and nobleness of nature, and the person of all others I would soonest trust or have to do with." Mr. C. Litton Falkner's Essay on *An Illustrious Cavalier*, and Lady Burghclere's *Life of the Duke of Ormonde*, are worthy records of his life. It is strange that no portrait exists of the Duchess of Ormonde—born in the same room as Lady Fanshawe was.

† With reference to Lady Fanshawe's escape from Cork to Kinsale, on 17 October, 1649, through the services of Colonel John Gifford, it may be noted that his family settled in Ireland and was subsequently resident at Aghern. He was born in 1603 and appears as a sergeant major (general) in Richard Fanshawe's list of 1640, and was no doubt the Captain Gifford whom the Earl of

Of the plague in Ireland Lord Ormonde wrote in 1650: "To all God's other judgements upon this Kingdom it hath pleased him to add that of a very raging pestilence, which hath already apparently gained the enemy Kilkenny and Kilmallock." According to the authority of Hardiman's *Galway*, 3700 people died of the plague in that town between July, 1649, and Lady-day, 1650. In 1614 Galway was described as built of "small, but fair and stately buildings; the fronts of the houses are all of hewn stone up to the top, garnished with fair battlements in a uniform course, as if the whole town had been built upon one model." In 1657 it was said of the place, "Poor Galway sitteth in the dust and no eye pitieth her. Her merchants were princes and great among the nations, but now the city which was full of people is solitary and very desolate."

In the previous year the Irish Council, noticing that the town was "very defensive both by art and nature" and consisted "of many noble buildings, uniform and most of them of marble . . . yet by reason of the late horrid rebellion and general waste then, and since made by the impoverished English inhabiting there, many of the houses" had "become very ruinous," recom-

Wimbledon noted at the worth of 3 or 4 other captains, in 1627. He was a commander of foot under Sir Thomas Fairfax at the capture of Wakefield in 1643, and according to Hyde's letter of 1653 had been one of the chief officers who kept the King out of Hull: on 2 August, 1649, he commanded the infantry of the Marquis of Ormonde at Rathmines when Colonel Jones defeated the Royalist Lord Lieutenant, Inchiquin being away in Munster, where it was anticipated Cromwell might land. In 1653 he was living at Ardmore and obtained a grant of lands from the Parliament, which was confirmed to him after the Restoration. In June, 1666, Lord Ossory reported on him, and his fellow actor in the Cork uprising, Colonel Townshend, as loyal supporters of the crown and each raising a company of foot, he described the former as a stout man and good officer and the latter as a rich man and with brains. Colonel Townshend was only 36 in 1649, and lived till 1692: he received no less than £40,000 for the destruction of his seat at Castle Townshend. *Carte* asserts that he was sent to Munster by Cromwell to work for the Irish interests there. Though Lady Fanshawe escaped from Cork, it appears from Cliffe's *History of the Irish Rebellion*, 1743, that the wife and family of Lord Inchiquin were captured and that he effected their release with much difficulty; and from the statement of a witness at the enquiry made on the fall of that place, it seems that the Bishop of Derry was actually taken prisoner too, but escaped. (Hyde severely criticises Gifford's vacillating conduct.)

mended that the loyal town of Gloucester should be allowed to make a plantation of it. This was attempted, but proved a complete failure. Mr. Bagnall adds in his *Ireland under the Stuarts*, that the old trade with Spain, interrupted by the war, never returned, and the city never recovered its prosperity.

Of the appearance of the Banshee at Lady Honora O'Brien's, it may be said with Walton, upon the record of an apparition to Dr. Donne, " This is a relation that will beget some wonder and well it may; for most of our world are at present possessed with an opinion that visions and miracles are ceased . . . and I am very well pleased to let every reader enjoy his own opinion." Lady Honora died in September, 1676, the year in which the *Memoirs* were transcribed, and was buried with her first husband at Englefield, Berks; but there is no memorial of her in the church there. She had married him at St. Andrews, Holborn, in 1656 and, as noted at p. 254, she married the Hon. Sir Robert Howard in 1666, after the death of Sir Francis Englefield.

Soon after Sir Richard's departure from Ireland, the Marquis of Ormonde wrote to Sir Edward Hyde and Lord Cottington, in Spain, about him and the state of Irish affairs, as follows (Carte, *Ormonde original letters*, 1739, Vol. II., 446):—" The misfortune of my being entangled in some business that allowed me not time to write to your Lordships when Mr. Fanshaw went hence, I should have accounted much greater if any other person had gone; but he was so perfect in the first transaction of the peace, in the success of the rebel arms, in the condition of the King's affairs before he went, and in the preparations which I think even before his going were making by a violent part of the clergy to shake off the King's authority, that if I had had time to write it had been little more than a credential to him; and that also I conceive was supplied both by his public interest in the King's business and your Lordships' particular knowledge of his zeal and abilities that are in him to observe what may tend most to it."

Of the third visit of Richard Fanshawe to Spain, with his wife and daughter Nan and sister-in-law, there is nothing to add to the account at p. 408-15 of the *Memoirs*, his stay in the country having lasted only six months. Anne Fanshawe well deserved the encomium which Sir T. Smythe wrote to Sir Dudley Carleton of that ambassador's wife in 1609, "that she will be contented to take such a voyage, deserves thanks for her love and praise for her valour." Another rival of hers in this respect was the wife of Sir Thomas Roe, who behaved with great courage when the ship on which they were sailing from Smyrna to Leghorn in 1628, was attacked by a Maltese Galley. The Turkish pirates once laid a plot to capture the Bishop of Malaga which was nearly successful: another person who was famous in the church, Isaac Barrow, had like Richard Fanshawe, to fight for the defence of his vessel in 1657.

Besides the instructions given Fanshawe from Hampton Court on 9 October, 1647 (*Memoirs*, p. 377), he had received later a letter from King Charles I., dated Newport, 7 October, 1648 (which was probably procured for him by Sir Philip Warwick, then in attendance on the King), upon his going into Ireland, and this confirms the date of his starting for that country. The letter is in Latin and refers to the credentials of 9 October previous, and explains that since that date the Resident to be, had been detained by certain weighty affairs of our son, the Prince of Wales, in which use had been made of his labour and service, and expresses a hope that a way is about to be found out of the terrible and long continued calamities of our Kingdom.

On $\frac{7}{17}$ April, Fanshawe wrote from Madrid to Mr. Long: "after a long and tedious voyage by sea and journey by land (for I disembarked at Malaga) I am now by God's blessing safely arrived in this Court." He wrote again to Long on 3 June and the tone of the correspondence between the two was always quite friendly, in spite of what Lady Fanshawe records on pp. 31 and 37 of the *Memoirs*. In the first letter

Fanshawe refers to his from Ireland to his correspondent, and expresses the hope that he will shortly receive a much desired answer, " and therein a further testimony of your continued care for me both for what concerns my relation to his Maties fleet and also my residence in this court, with such countenance and support from our Royal Master as besides the comfort to myself (being the thing which is least material) may the better enable me to his Majesty." In the 2nd letter dated 3 June but which was not received till 12 September, by which time the writer was in France, Sir Richard makes the same request, and mentions that Sir Edward Hyde had received a letter from Long saying that he (Fanshawe) must be arrived in Spain or cast away, as the person to whom he had entrusted his letters on leaving Ireland had arrived in the Low Countries, but containing " no little clause added of instruction and present light for me, wherewith to stay my stomach in case I were arrived." Fanshawe also asked for " necessary authorities and credentials to qualify me in this court," adding, " notwithstanding I do not as yet foresee anything that is likely to hinder my journey to attend his Majesty personally, as I advertised in my last "—this letter unluckily is not forthcoming.

Sir Edward Hyde and Lord Cottington lived in the Calle de Alcala at Madrid, not far from Siete Chimeneas where Fanshawe had no doubt resided with Lord Aston, and where he was to reside again 14 years later as Ambassador. Of Lord Cottington, Fuller recorded: " he raised himself by his natural strength without any artificial advantage, having his parts above his learning, and his experience above his parts, his industry above his experience, and (some will say) his success above all."

The Fanshawes could not have met Dr. Beale* at Oxford as suggested on p. 412 of the *Memoirs*, as *Dugdale* records that he did not arrive there on release from his imprisonment till June, 1645. During the time that

* Dr. Beale left the seal ring, he usually wore, to Lord Hatton.

Fanshawe was at Madrid, Marmaduke Rawdon, distinguished from others of the same name by the description of the traveller, was also there, and according to Mr. Tregelles Hoddesdon, he mentions the murder of Anthony Ascham (*Memoirs*, p. 68). As it has been objected that Sir Edward Hyde spoke of this murder in too light terms, it may be mentioned as illustrative of the spirit of the times, that the Duke de Medina de las Torres, with whom Richard Fanshawe had so much to do in 1664-66, refers to it as a "loable ejemplo de lealtad."

The return of the Fanshawes from Spain to Paris in September-November, 1650 calls for no special notice: Evelyn journeyed down the Loire from Orleans to Blois in the summer of 1644 and met Queen Henrietta Maria at the latter place on 10 August, fresh from her flight from Exeter and England. The stay of the Fanshawes in Paris was evidently very short, as Lady Fanshawe had been seven months in Hunsdon House before she moved to Queen Street, and her second daughter named Elizabeth, was born there on 24 June, 1651.

The mission to Scotland of Sir Richard as he now was, for his Baronetcy is dated 2 September, 1650, must have been proposed very soon after he reached Paris, as Sir Edward Hyde refers to it in a letter of 19 December from Madrid, observing that Fanshawe was a very honest and discreet man and designed by the late King for attendance on the Duke of York: it would seem from the correspondence of the time that he went to Scotland originally as an emissary from the Duke, with whom he must have been six weeks or more in Holland, but this may have been merely a pretext to get him there without the knowledge of the person whose place he was to take. This was Sir Robert Long, whom he thus succeeded on a second occasion no more happy than the first, so far as the humiliations and difficulties which the Secretary must have encountered, were concerned. No fresh information regarding Sir Richard's services in that capacity has come to light.

In the march to Worcester, the King and his Scottish army passed Myerscough where one of the Fanshawe estates in Lancashire was situated. Worcester was an unfortunate selection for a stand by the King's army, as the place had been beseiged by Colonel Rainsborough from 21 May-23 July, 1646, and no doubt many officers in Cromwell's army were well acquainted with the ground round it, and the facilities offered for attack. Besides the records quoted at p. 422 of the *Memoirs*, regarding Sir Richard Fanshawe being made prisoner the day after the battle—at Newport—his capture is noted in Francis Egglefield's *Monarchy Restored* and in Dr. Bates' Latin work *Elenchus motuum nuperorum in Anglia*. The former states that when the Earls of Derby and Lauderdale and Sir Richard Fanshawe were taken, the Duke of Buckingham and others escaped into the Chesswardine Woods north of Newport. This party had separated from the King at Kniver Heath north of Kidderminster when he turned north-east to Boscobel, and finding their way north barred by Ludlow's cavalry at Newport, tried to push round the place on the west side. The place of the skirmish which thereupon ensued, is marked on the Ordnance Survey map 500 yards west of the Market Place and Parish church and on the south side of the Shropshire Union canal: when that was dug, a number of bones of those killed on the occasion, were brought to light again.

There is some mistake of Lady Fanshawe's (*Memoirs*, p. 80), in the statement that Lady Denham of Borstall excused herself, on the ground that she had no sons at home, for her inability to provide the captive cavalier with an outfit of under linen. Lady (Penelope) Denham, who was daughter of Lord Wenman and widow of Sir John Denham (died in 1634), had no sons: their daughter Mary married Lawrence Banastre in 1632, and Borstall*

* About 1430, Borstall had come through a female to the Redes, from the de la Poles, and in the 4th generation after, it went to Thomas Denham or Dynham who died in 1562. Thomas was apparently the Denham who received half of the manor of Norton, Derbyshire, through another wife, Joanna, daughter of John Ormonde, which her son sold to John Bullock. The statement

was then settled on her. Lady Denham lived till 1672, and the estate passed through her daughter to one William Lewis, and through his grand-daughter to the Aubrey family (Lipscombe's *History of Buckinghamshire*).

It may be again remarked that Sir Richard was extremely fortunate in escaping with only 2 months confinement after the battle of Worcester, for by an Act of Parliament passed in March, 1649, any person attempting to revive or set up again the royal office, was declared to be guilty of high treason, and Sir Richard, as Secretary to Charles II., was a very marked supporter of his attempt to recover the throne. It is probable that (with Lord Hopton), he was held in high esteem by the leaders of the popular side; but no doubt his connection with Cromwell, who like himself was descended from a daughter of Sir Thomas Mirfyn (see p. 107) must have stood him in good stead, and clearly *his* devoted Althea did everything a woman could to further that interest in his behalf.

When once he was freed from close confinement, until he was allowed to proceed to France in October, 1658, his time was spent with his wife as follows: 1652 London, Bath, and Bayfordbury; 1653, into the summer of 1654, Tankersley Park, Yorkshire, rest of 1654, Hamerton (Lady Bedell's), and London; 1655, Frognall (Sir Philip Warwick's), and London; 1656, London and Bengeo, adjoining Ware Park; 1657 to the summer of 1658, Bengeo, Bath and the Priory at Ware, at which house the news of the death of the Protector on 3 September, reached them.

The original correspondence between Sir Richard Fanshawe and the Earl of Strafford* regarding the

in the *Verney Papers* published by the Camden Society, that the Judge, Sir John Denham, father of the poet who wrote the complimentary verses upon Sir Richard's translation of the *Pastor Fido*, owned Borstal, is a mistake.

* He was not *de facto* Earl of Strafford at this time, that title having been forfeited by the attainder of his father. No doubt Sir Richard knew him in Ireland in 1639-40, and perhaps he may have had educational charge of him there by request of the Lord Lieutenant.

lease of Tankersley Park, existed among the *Heathcote MSS.* before they were scattered. The lease bore the date of March, 1653, but the correspondence began at the end of the previous year, and on 16 December the Earl wrote to Sir George Wentworth that he intended to lend the house to Sir Richard "unto whom," he added, "I shall rest confident you will upon all occasions afford those civilities and kindness proper to a gentleman that comes a stranger into our country, and from my friends to one of whom I have a very particular esteem." Later, replying to a letter from Sir Richard from Bayford, the Earl wrote, "You may always be most confident my desires have been and always shall be that you may be most at your convenience, you and yours." The lease was for 21 years at a rental of £60 *p.a.*: among the terms of it the 280 deer in the Park were to have hay in winter and there was to be a right of gystment or pasturage, free or for a fixed price, for 24 mares and horses. In December, 1653, the Earl made an allowance to his tenant for building outwalls for gardens, no doubt those mentioned in the *Memoirs*. In his Ode on the King's proclamation in 1630, Richard Fanshawe wrote:

> "Plant trees you may and see them shoot
> Up with your children, to be serv'd
> To your clean Boards, and the fair'st fruit
> To be preserv'd,"

and at Tankersley he put his precept into practice.

Though the Fanshawes left this place in 1654 on the death of their daughter Nan, the lease still remained in force, and in 1657 there was a slight disagreement over the Earl being misled into making a claim of arrears on account of gystment. This was satisfactorily settled, Sir Richard receiving £500 for giving up the lease of the residence which was needed for a dower house, and the Earl promising him a brace of bucks each summer and 2 brace of does each winter "out of the true sense I have of his ingenuous and disportive carriage thro'out the whole business."

Probably the brace of bucks presented by Sir Richard

Margaret Fanshawe (1653-1705), daughter of Sir Richard Fanshawe

by Theodore Russel

Valence House Museum

Ann Fanshawe (b.1654), daughter of Sir Richard Fanshawe

by Theodore Russel

Valence House Museum

Fanshawe to Cambridge University on his election as the Member of Parliament for that constituency in 1661, came from Tankersley Park.

As noted at p. 47, Richard Fanshawe was concerned during the years 1652-8 in the attempts to straighten out the financial liabilities of his wife's father, Sir John Harrison, and the Stoke Rochford papers relating to these, show that in March, 1656, Sir Richard was residing, perhaps only temporarily, in Little Queen St., a residence omitted by Lady Fanshawe from the Memoirs.

The illness from which Lady Fanshawe and her husband suffered in 1657-8 is conjectured to have been influenza; special details of the attacks of it are given in the *Verney Papers* and in the *Life of Marmaduke Rawdon.*

Sir John Denham was granted a pass in 1658 to travel abroad with the Earl of Pembroke, and perhaps Sir Richard Fanshawe, the elder poet of the two, was chosen to go in his place, since we know that the latter did go to Paris with the Earl's son at that date. Considering the line taken by the Earl in the politics of the day, it seems somewhat strange to find him on friendly terms with Sir Richard.

We now come to some of the most interesting papers which have freshly come to light in connection with Sir Richard Fanshawe, viz., his original letters of 1659 to Sir Edward Hyde, contained in Vols. 61-67 of the *Clarendon MSS.* in the Bodleian Library. These are 13 in number dating from 6 June to 12 December, and complete the correspondence in the *Heathcote Historical MSS.*, noted at p. 432 of the *Memoirs.* The letters were written under the disguise of the pseudonym of G. Francis; but as they are all in Sir Richard's unmistakable autograph, and several have the impression of his seal with the family coat of arms, and one bears the scarcely erased signature of "Ric. F.," it is difficult to see what advantage was expected from this semi cryptic proceeding. It appears from Hyde's letter of 10 May, the earliest in the series, that a communication of 4

October from Sir Richard, written *before* he left England,* and which Hyde remarks would have been likely to have put an end to his voyage if it had been intercepted, did not reach the Chancellor's hands till about the end of March. Having learnt before then that his correspondent was in Paris, and not having heard from him again, Hyde wrote to ask if it was permissible to correspond with him while he was abroad; and learning that it was, proceeded to do so, and to rate him for not having previously asserted his claim to the post of Secretary of State, as recorded in the notes to the *Memoirs*.

From Hyde's letter of 31 May it appears that Sir Richard had been away from Paris, no doubt accompanying his pupil, Lord Herbert, on some excursion and was about to return.

In his letter of 20 June, Sir Richard gives the following account of his literary works, in reply to an enquiry of Hyde's of the 14th *idem*:—"What I have most studied ever since my captivitie hath been foreign languages; and the most that I have published other men's matter: viz., a portingall heroic poem of Luis de Camoens, englisht; and Fletcher's faithfull shepherdesse, latinised—I thought them both very unworthy of your lordship's sight, not only because ill written but ill printed, being at times when I could not be present to overlooke the Presse.

I have by me unpublisht a traduction out of Castilian of Querer por solo querer.

Thus idle and frivolous have I been of later years, and perhaps otherwise I had not been now at liberty. Cautum as well as dulce est desipere in loco." As Sir Richard does not mention the translation of the *Fiestas de Aranjuez*, that was probably a work of his Embassy in Spain. The omission of the *translation of Horace* published in 1652, confirms the conjecture on p. 230 of the Memoirs, that this was an earlier work of his.

* His bonds were released on 15 October, and presumably he went abroad shortly after that date.

He gives as his address in Paris, the Rue de Boucherie, which is not to be identified. From Hyde's letter of 20 September in which he refers to one of his correspondent's of the 12th (not forthcoming), it appears that Lady Fanshawe had reached Paris before the earlier date.* Sir Richard does not refer to her in a letter of the 19 September, but on 4 October mentions her, as his "late-come friend" who "returns most humble service and devotion to your Lordship and your relations." Her arrival must therefore have been in the first ten days of September, not in June as recorded at page 90 of the *Memoirs;* and her son Richard was taken from her by death just about a month after that date. In a letter of 7 November Sir Richard thanks Hyde for his "condolement of a sensible loss I have lately susteynd, so sensible a one that I have no will to repeat it, much less to exaggerate it by many perticular circumstances which are not ordinarily found in the like cases." The poor boy who was carried off by the smallpox in his 12th year, appears with his father in the picture reproduced at p. 4 of the *Memoirs.*† Sir Richard's last letter of 12

* Henry Neville, through whom Lady Fanshawe sought to obtain a passport from Wallingford House, is often mentioned in the travels of Cosmo de Medici, whose acquaintance he had made in Florence and on whose staff he was, during the Prince's travels in England. In 1679 he was accused of borrowing money from the Jesuits and asked leave to go abroad again. Later in life he wrote "*Plato Redivivus,*" and "*Discourses concerning government.*" The latter form a weighty and sensible treatise in support of the gentry, steadily recruited from the wealthier middle classes; and recommending Parliamentary committees to exercise, with the King, the powers of making peace and war; controlling the army; and appointing all high officials of state; these powers being too great for the King to exercise alone. On his death in 1694 Neville was buried at Waltham St. Lawrence, near Billingbear.

† Dr. Cosins who buried him (*Memoirs*, p. 215), wrote in his personal defence against the charge that he had improperly associated with the French Protestants in Paris, "I have buried divers of our people in Charenton, and they permit us to make use of their peculiar and decent cemetary here in Paris for that purpose, which if they did not we should be forced to bury our dead in a ditch." The Paris Protestant cemetery of this date, called unkindly des prétendus reformés, and later "Cimetière de la Charité autrefois des Protestants," appears on the maps of Paris of the late XVII. and early XVIII. centuries in the Rue des Saints Pères, where its site is occupied at the present day by the School of Engineering (*Ponts et Chaussées*), over and against the well known Hôpital de la Charité, situated a little to the west of the Abbey of St. Germain des Prés.

December was written subsequently to his meeting King Charles again after 8 years at Colombes, where the King arrived, according to a letter of Mr. Percy Church, on 5 December, from the conference at the Isle des Faisans; "I find indeed my master," wrote his servant "(without flatterie to him or the companie he hath kept) improved every way far beyond my expectation, tho' it was very great; to me gratious as much beyond my hopes; and that best of friends [the Marquis of Ormonde] whom your Lordship not naming hath sufficiently disguised as to any other reader than myself by styling him mine (the disproportion between us claiming a title paramount to that) as kind as your lordship or my selfe can wish." From enclosures to this letter it appears that Sir Richard had pressed his claims to the promised post of Secretary of State, on the King, and had sought to get a dormant grant of that in succession to the Earl of Bristol, the grant to be inoperative unless the King should be pleased to summon him and declare it, and unless the grantee should make a gift of £2000 to the King. Such a proposal must not be judged by the standards of a later age. In the Stuart times, as in Oriental Courts, every appointment was subject to a payment to the Crown, or to some patron to whom the crown assigned the patronage, even the appointments of Ambassadors and Judges. The correspondence of the times is as full of records of such transactions, as the records of the Great Mughal would have been of the presentation of "nazzars."* Between the date of Sir Richard's com-

* Lord Sandwich for instance recorded in his diary on 24 May, 1668: "Thinking opportunity was not to be lost to see if I could gett any Thinge more out of this court while present, I determined to go and declare my resentment to the Count of Pennaranda and did so this day." The Duke told him that if the Treaty with Portugal could have been secured without conceding the title of King, the Queen of Spain would have paid him 70,000 pieces of eight and Mr. Godolphin 30,000, and that Lady Sandwich was to receive a jewel of 25,000 ducats over and above what her husband received. Father Duffi had told him in September, 1667, that Sir Richard Fanshawe was to have received 150,000 ducats, and that Lady Fanshawe received a jewel of 8000 ducats while at the Court and 2000 ducats on leaving, all of which Lady Fanshawe herself openly records.

Sir Richard Fanshawe's personal seal

Private family collection

Replica of silver patten presented by Sir Richard Fanshawe to St George's Chapel, Windsor, in 1661 in his capacity as Chancellor of the Order of the Garter. This limited edition replica was produced by Harrods in 1977 to commemorate the Silver Jubilee of Queen Elizabeth II.

Private collection

munication to Hyde in May, 1659, reminding him of the King's engagement to confer the office of Secretary of State on him, which the King remembered no more than anything that was done the day he was born (*Memoirs*, p. 432), and the meeting of the King and his ex-Secretary at Colombes in December, Charles II., with characteristic effrontery and ingratitude, had promised the post to Sir Henry Bennet at Fuente Rabia.

When Lady Fanshawe returned from her last mission to England to bring resources to her husband, she no doubt travelled by " Trek " boat—as described by Evelyn —to Dunkirk, Bruges, Brussels, Breda, and the Hague. The presence of her daughter Mary, in the picture painted by Teniers, shows that she also was brought back by her mother; the fourth daughter Nan remaining in England. This picture is now in the possession of Admiral of the Fleet Sir A. D. Fanshawe, G.C.B.

The narrative in the memoirs, of the proceedings of Sir Richard Fanshawe and his wife at the time of the Restoration and during her two years residence in London, is unusually full and does not need addition.

It is curious how Shakespeare, in his Henry V., anticipated the popular acclamation of an English King at Dover and at London. How closely joy and sorrow are related in life is instanced by the fact that the wife of Thomas Fanshawe, later 2nd Viscount, with whom Lady Fanshawe viewed the King's progress through London on 29 May, was buried at Ware on 14 June. The warrant for the installation of Sir Richard in place of the Earl of Bristol, at the Garter Investiture of 16 April, 1661, is in the Bodleian—(*Ashmolean MSS.*, 1114, *F.* 24). It bears the date of 16 March and recites his nomination, "at the request of the countess of Bristoll in behalfe of the Earle her husband," as possessing all the qualifications for such a deputation: curiously enough it is addressed to Sir Richard as Knight only, and not as Baronet too.

From the *Heathcote MSS.* it appears that Lady Fanshawe accompanied her husband, with Sir Andrew

King, to his port of embarcation in September, 1661, and that they returned again to Deal from Canterbury, on hearing he was detained in the Downs; but found on arriving there that he had sailed again. *The Princess*, which carried him to Portugal, appears in Dirk Stoop's plate, of the Duke of York meeting the Queen at sea under escort of the Earl of Sandwich—*Memoirs*, p. 451.

A real compliment was paid to Sir Richard as a Portuguese scholar, by Don Francisco Manuel de Mello, who in February, 1666, sent to the Ambassador, then seeking at Benavente to persuade the Portuguese to accept the terms of peace proposed by Spain, a copy of his *Obras metricas* (and) *morales* in return for the Englishman's translation of the *Lusiado*. Among the same MSS. is also a record of a very fulsome Latin Oration delivered before the wedding-emissary, in the Library of the English College at Lisbon, and of a set of verses recited in his honour which ended with the following lines:—

> "Take then a pencill and a temple rayse
> Transcending Spaynes and your Escuriall's prayse.
> Then in it place the Queen and on each side
> Rayse altars to the virtue of the Bride.
> By her inthroned in armour all complete
> Join hand in hand her bridegroom Charles the Great,
> And whilst amazement makes the beholders dumb
> Warble a sweet epithalamium
> Unto the royal pair; then mounting higher
> From Poets fury to the Prophets Quire,
> Unroll the good yet dark decrees of fate
> And read these nuptials truly fortunate."*

The house in Portugal Row which Lady Fanshawe continued to occupy whilst Sir Richard was away from September to the end of December, 1661, was situated

* Dr. Heaven who accompanied Sir Richard to Lisbon in 1661—the date of whose application for leave to the Provost of Eton was printed wrongly 31 October instead of 27 August (*Memoirs*, p. 454)—was a fellow of Clare College, Cambridge, with Dr. Henry Newce, nephew of Sir Richard. When he applied for a Canonry of Windsor in June 1660, his claim to consideration was endorsed by Sir Richard and countersigned by Bishops Sheldon and Morley. The first certified that he had an intimate acquaintance from many years past with the petitioner who had been engaged in diligences of more than usual hazard in the King's interests with Sir Robert Shirley of Staunton Harold, who died under confinement in the Tower.

my Lord & Husband. I shall take it for a particular favour, that yr Matie for my sake would
be pleased to bestow upon the Bearer hereof
Sr Richard Fanshaw some considerable office
in my Household, the wch he himselfe may
propose unto yr Matie, being such as yr Matie
shall find him capable of, for the well that
his deportment hath appeared to this court, &
the cheerfullnesse wherewth he undertakes this
Voyage at my comand for the service of this
crowne. And likewise that yr Matie would be
pleased to graunt unto his wife Donna Anna, the
office to be that woman of my bed-chamber,
unto whom it belongs also to be Lady of the
Jewells; and that this favour may be gran[ted]
her, as well for the services of her Husband,
whom yr Matie doth so graciously owne, as for
her much vertue, & particular qualifications
wch I am informed are found in her person
for the discharge of that ~~[illegible]~~ Imployment.

Draft letter in Richard Fanshawe's hand.
A request for offices in Queen Catherine's household for Sir Richard Fanshawe and his wife, to be copied by the Queen in her own hand.

November 1661 - Lisbon

LBBD Archives at Valence House

Engraving of a portrait of Sir Richard Fanshawe (1666)

LBBD Archives at Valence House

at the east end of the south side of Lincoln's Inn Fields, which was the only part of that side on which houses had then been built, and the site of it is now occupied by No. 35. On her return from Spain in November, 1666, she lived in Lady Middlesex's house, now No. 13 included in the Soane Museum, and later, in 1673, she resided for a time in No. 26, nearly at the east end of the north side of the Fields.*

The Lady who was appointed to be chief of the Bed-women to the Queen, with precedence in place and salary, was the wife of Sir Henry Wood of Hackney, who had been Treasurer to Queen Henrietta Maria and became Clerk of the Board of Green Cloth on the Restoration. That Lady Fanshawe made no special appeals to the Queen, after her return to England, shows clearly how little her influence was held to be. It may be remembered that the remains of the poor Royal Lady were removed from the Belem Monastery to the Royal mausoleum in the church of San Vincente, Lisbon, on 25 March, 1914; the presence of the British minister on the occasion being the last honour paid to her.

In a letter dated 1 November, 1662 (*Portugal S.P.V.*) King Affonso, in accepting the mediation of Charles II., recommended that Don Ricardo Fanshon should be appointed commissioner for the purpose.

An interesting account of the route of Sir Richard and his family to Plymouth, is given, in the reverse direction, in the *Travels of Cosmo de Medici*, Prince of Tuscany, in which Sir John Skelton and Sir Richard Edgcumbe are mentioned; the illustrations of the book give interesting views of most of the places at which they halted, views which are much more effective in the copies

* Many persons mentioned in the *Memoirs* also lived in Lincoln's Inn Fields—Lord Strangford at No. 34 (north side); the son of Sir Philip Warwick (1660-75) at No. 40; and the Countess of Sunderland and her husband Mr. Robert Smythe at No. 42—both on the site of the present College of Surgeons (s. side); Lord Crewe in No. 52; and his son in law the Earl of Sandwich in No. 57-8 (w. side). Later on, Sir Thomas Heathcote, ancestor of the owner of the Fanshawe MSS., lived at No. 13; and Mr. Justice Wilson (died 1793), father of the wife of Admiral Sir Arthur Fanshawe, K.C.B., at No. 15.

of the original drawings in the British Museum than in the printed reproductions. Gay, in a poem addressed to Lord Burlington, also describes the journey from London to Exeter.

With reference to Lady Fanshawe's statement that the arms of the Ambassador were left at his lodgings, it may be noted that Machyn records in his diary that the "imbassadur to the Frenche kyng the yerle of Bedford" had "iij dosen of logyng (lodging) skochyons" (escutcheons) prepared for him; and that the coats of arms left by Sir Henry Wotton and Sir Philip Sidney are mentioned in *Pearsall Smith's Life of Wotton*. Dr. Baylie, Dean of Salisbury and President of St. John's College, Oxford, was buried in the College chapel, where his effigy may still be seen; the inscription below it states:—"in integrum restitutus quamvis jubente rege, poscente collegi Prerogativa, flagitante Ecclesia, id unum sibi contra commune votum, et publicam utilitatem indulgens Episcopale, mutare noluit." The beautiful Tudor Hall of Cotele, from which his cousin Colonel Piers Edgcumbe came to meet Sir Richard, is charmingly illustrated in Mr. N. M. Condy's book published in 1850.

There were a number of country seats, "quintas," near Belem—a very famous one in later times was that of the Marquis of Marialva, in which the Spanish flags captured at the battle of Elvas in 1659, were still hanging in 1787.

The *Heathcote MSS* include a letter written in French to the Portuguese Secretary, Don Antonio de Sousa de Macedo, by Sir Richard, the day before his public reception at Lisbon on $\frac{18}{28}$ September. Part of this may be quoted as a specimen of his French style:—"N'ayant pas presenté mes credentials au Roi je ne commence poynt encore d'agir en persone publique et de fayre mon office vers sa majesté. Neanmoins les affayres de ceste Corone estant si pressans au regard de Troupes Anglaises, je m'addresse à vous comme votre ami, que je suis particulier et tres fidelle serviteur, pour vous fayre savoir ce que m'assure maintenant Mons. le Conte d'Insiquin (et la chose n'est que trop manifeste mesme de soi) les mauvaises consequences qu'il peuve avoir si les remedes ne devancent les ceremonies de ma reception et audience publique en payant les dits troupes le temps passé sans remise et les assurant l'avenir conformement aux articles deja arrestés avec le dit Monsieur le Compte." In a letter from Queen Luisa to King Charles II. of the date of 22 October (*P.R.O.*), the former wrote of Sir Richard " el hase como fiel vasallo de V. Mag[d] y en todo se muestra digno deste empleo." Two important matters were reported to England by Sir Richard early in 1663—one on 12 March, that Count Schomberg had without any reference to him been placed at the head of the British troops in Portugal, the fidelity of their officers, suffering from heavy grievances of arrears of pay, being suspected—the other of 17 March, that he had accompanied the Queen on her retreat to the Xabrejas Convent, constituted by her on the Tagus bank about a mile above the city of Lisbon. Apparently the Ambassador continued to reside in the Quinta of the Duke of Aveiro throughout his stay in Lisbon up to the middle of August, 1663. Maynard, Consul General of Lisbon, had been appointed as local British representative in 1656 by the Protector: he was originally a Plymouth merchant, and after the Restoration had a hard job to maintain his authority with the Royalist traders of the place.

Of the beauty of the aspect of Lisbon the proverb runs:—

Quien no ha visto Lisboa
No ha visto cosa boa

and Camoens wrote of his loved city:—

E tu nobre Lisboa que no mundo
Facilmente das outras es princessa

which Fanshawe neatly translates:—

" And thou fair Lisbon, worthy to be crown'd
Of all the cities of the world the Queen."

In an important letter of 1 May, 1663, to Sir Henry Bennet, after speaking of a letter of the Secretary's as " the first to reskue me from utter darkness since I left

Hampton Court" (eight months previously), Sir Richard spoke of a conference on Peace between himself, the Conde de Castel Melhor, the Archbishop of Lisbon, the Marques de Nyzza, and the Secretary Antonio de Macedo de Sousa, at which the Portuguese had expressed great gratitude for the offer of mediation by the King of England; but regretted that the King would not guarantee the peace if made, as the King of Spain might break it at any time on the plea that he was not bound to keep any terms with rebels. Marshall Schomberg was going to the front that day from a sick-bed; "The King with the advice of his council hath voted himself to go in person to the Army, at least to draw towards it; but there wants yet the popular assent, the people claiming the privilege by the Juez del Pueblo (which is much in the nature of Tribunus populi, and hath signified a great matter in some former ages) to forbid the banns in cases of less hazard than that by a ceremony of tying a ribbon about his maties leg." This forbidding did not apparently take place, as the letter of Sir Richard offering to accompany King Affonso to the front, before the idea of that was given up on the occurrence of the Lisbon riots on 25 May, is dated 19 May; two letters of the Earl of Peterburgh (as he spells his name), of the dates of 22 and 29 May, 1663, in the *Heathcote* MSS.—the latter referring "to the loss,* which I pray God repair and preserve my good ladye to your comfort"—must be those referred to by Lady Fanshawe on p. 112 of the *Memoirs*: it is beyond all doubt that she had the papers in this collection by her when she compiled her work.

Of the Conde de Villa Flor, the Portuguese commander at the battle of Evora, fought on 29 May/8 June, Schomberg wrote "no one saw him during the battle at all"; but the *Relacion Mercurio de la famosa y memorabile Vitoria*, in the *Heathcote MSS.*, loyally recorded "él lo mando, él lo peleo, él lo gano (he was the commander, he was the soldier, he was the victor)—su nombre serà eterno triunfante de Olvido como de los Castellanos." The narrative

* Of the son prematurely born at Lisbon on 26 June.

naturally gives limited praise to the French—which it places first—and English troops, and states the latter refused quarter. A note by Sir Richard as to this, records that this "was in the heate thereof the English being provoked before and to the battayle by the Spanyards," but afterwards they did, as the Secretary himselfe told him, give quarter.

On the *Mercurio Portuguez* of March, 1663, forwarded to Sir Henry Bennet (who became Secretary of State in 1662), Sir Richard wrote—"this gazette speaks something of the treaty between Spain and Portugal, as I presume everyone will do more or less so long as any show of life shall remain therein." On referring to the *Mercurios* of May, Sir Richard wrote: "Portugal is but a novice at this trade using it as yet only monthly, and that on compulsion too because the Spanish Gazette belittles them and those of all other nations neglects them, whose proper metier is to act what foreigners (more addicted to the pen than to the sword) write." It is the expression of their own first gazette of the month of January.

In his letter of $\frac{3}{13}$ July briefly noted at p. 123 *Heathcote MSS.*, Sir Richard wrote to the Secretary of State, "all the poynts of my negotiation in this court being brought to a head and issue which is ready for his Maties clear survey whereupon to give his future Royall orders or final decision, I have determined (God willing) by the first of next month stylo loci to sett sayle in person for England, by virtue of an instruction from his Matie, a copy whereof is herewith enclosed likewise, and which I think it my duty and advantage to acquaint your Hon^{r} with, lest not having known thereof before I should incurr, though it were but one day, secret censure from yr. Hon^{r} of proceeding thereunto without due warrant and circumspection, being sensible what first impressions are. . . . This being in generall I doubt not when I come of rendering such particular reasons why I come as shall for this one time save the forfeit of my discretion" (*State Papers Foreign, Portugal*, Bundle 6, P.R.O.).

This is the last letter from Lisbon but one, which is dated five days later, in the *State Records* in the Public Record office.

The Fanshawes returned to England in the *Reserve* commanded by Capt. Holmes.* Colonel Norwood, who was concerned with the latter in the affront offered in the Bull ring, must also have been their companion, as the *Heathcote Papers* show that he was received at Court at Bath in the middle of September with Sir Richard. The return of the Ambassador was not approved at home, though he had general permission to leave Portugal if the King's affairs required this (*Heathcote MSS.*, p. 131) and orders were sent dated 25 July (*Bodleian, Tanner MSS.*) directing him to remain, and even to go back to Lisbon should they meet him at sea; but they missed him and were probably a cause of much consternation when received, to his Secretary, Lyonell Fanshawe, who was left behind again as in the winter of 1661. In a letter of $\frac{20}{30}$ August Consul Maynard reported that Sir Richard had sailed from Lisbon $\frac{13}{23}$, and that on the $\frac{19}{29}$, six days after his departure, a ketch had arrived with a packet for him, and no one in Lisbon having power to open it, the ketch was returning to England with it.

The Ambassador recorded one memo. at Bath on the subject of his return in which he said, "I am humbly of opinion that my resort at this time to your Royall presence is not only not prejudicial but highly conducing and necessary towards the ends (of your Majesty's interests), and that in sundry respects, nothing doubting that the same will be so apparent to your majesty daily more and more when the maine of my papers . . . shall all be at hand," and in another later in September at Whitehall, he wrote how "the tottering condition of the crown and nation was beyond expectation of all the world but themselves (who never yet in their gravest extremities

* It was Holmes who brought General Montague's letter of the loyal determination of the Fleet, to Breda on $\frac{2}{12}$ May, 1660. He was knighted at Deptford in the spring of 1666. A marble effigy of him, said to have been converted from a statue of Louis XIV. captured at sea, still stands in the church at Yarmouth, Isle of Wight, for all the world to see.

despaired of a miracle . . .) converted to that universal jubilee in which I left them,'' and which made an occasion favourable for the mediation of peace between the crowns of Portugal and Spain, the Portuguese king desiring and urging his, the Ambassador's, appointment to Madrid with this object.* These reasons were no doubt ultimately accepted, as Sir Richard was honoured by the appointment to be Privy Councillor early in the following month; and if he had not effected in Lisbon all that was hoped of his mission he had obtained a payment of part of the Queen's dowry, and had insisted on the surrender of Bombay, and most important of all, had kept the British troops in the Portuguese service true to their salt, in spite of the most abominable neglect and ill treatment by the Portuguese Crown. Personally, the ambassador had been disgracefully treated in the matters of instructions from home, the first despatches he received reaching him at the end of March, six months after he left England; and of payment of his salary and allowances which were always heavily in arrears; and if any government servants could have exceeded those of the Spanish Government in stiff-neckedness, jealousies and ignorance, they were those of Affonso VI.†

Before proceeding to Lisbon he had recorded a full memo. of his views upon the situation in Portugal which he left with the Lord Chancellor, and which very probably went no farther, such was the official procedure of those days. This is in his own hand writing among the *Heathcote* MSS., and ended with the statement that the suggestions made in it were not to counsell his majesty, but to enable the Ambassador " to know the better how to govern himselfe in the imployment upon which he goes. The rather because your ma^tie knows he was not

* It may be recorded here that all attempts to ascertain if any records relating to the Embassy of Sir Richard Fanshawe, still exist in the State archives of Portugal, have proved wholly ineffectual.

† Possibly the Count of Castel Melhor should be exempted for the full stigma of this, Sir Robert Southwell recording of him " it was a miracle how he did keep things cemented together so long . . . the public voice accusing the extent of the charge he held and voting it down as exhorbitant and fit to be extinguished."

ambitious of this honour (tho' ten times his Betters might justly be so) preferring as to himself his quiet at home in his own declining Age, and after many storms of fortune both here and Abroad, with the advantage and comfort of a frequent accesse to your Royall presence, before any that can accrew him thereby, unless he may imploy his absence in being someway instrumentall to bring things to passe upon which your majestie setts your heart." One of these things the Ambassador accepted as quite clear, viz.: the desire that "the crowne of Portugal should be established in a flourishing peace and quietness severed from that of Castille."

Spain seemed to be setting the whole of her extended monarchy—now at liberty from all other quarrels—upon recovering the game with Portugal, and the Ambassador evidently considered it doubtful if the latter were sufficiently at unity to maintain her position, unless England were to make a speedy and powerful diversion by a Royal Fleet, or by the garrison at Tangier, or by menace of such force combined with specified considerable advantages to Spain. If this were not feasible (and of course it meant ultimate war with Spain), and if Portugal could not be saved otherwise (and it was questionable if her ruin might not be caused by internal treachery), the King of England might propose mediation on the basis that the King of Portugal should give up his title to that country, and should remain King of Brazil (a suggestion curiously paralled by the action of the Crown of Portugal in 1806), Goa, etc., the three powers forming an offensive and triple defensive league "against the suspected, or at least possible, combination and disturbing arts of more neighbouring nations, whose power by land and sea is vastly increased since the time that Queen Elizabeth in her wisdom found reason to uphold them against the Spanish greatnesse," or if "that infirm prince" the Infante shd. happen to die, perhaps (the Ambassador suggested) the King of Spain might be induced to betrothe his daughter to the King of Portugal instead of to the Emperor of Germany.

Even if Portugal were re-united with Spain the latter would never be in that condition it was in Queen Elizabeth's time to aspire to universal monarchy. Apparently no instructions were sent to the Ambassador on any of these points, and he clearly received no real support in the matters essential for the protection of the Portuguese crown, Lord Clarendon, writing to him openly, on 12 April, 1663 (*Heathcote* MSS, p. 75), "we have no money to send fleets or troops on adventures, nor can anybody imagine that the burden of a war of Portugal can be sustained upon the weak shoulders of the Crown of England. The King hath—with difficulty enough—been able to set out a fleet now to assist that kingdom, but if care be not taken there for payment of the remainder of the portion, the King will have little encouragement or—in truth—ability to continue that expense." The victory of Evora was therefore as much a miracle for the continuance of the policy of Charles II. towards Portugal as for the salvation of the Portuguese crown. In submitting to King Charles, King Affonso's and Queen Luisa's letters of 15 August, 1663, urging his appointment to negotiate a peace with Spain (*Heathcote* MSS., p. 131), Sir Richard recorded—(it is not quite clear if this part of the draft was actually incorporated in his memorial)—that he came "not uninvited or unimportuned to this mediation by the King of Portugall; who so far from repenting of this application, when his ma[tie] was assured (as he thought) of the King of Spayne's death, that receiving intelligence thereof after I was embarked and immediately to sett sayle he commanded mee on shore agaiyne upon that occasion to let me know he was then more of the same mind than formerly and to give me a new letter to the Marquess of Sande to the same purpose; but both the one and the other with so much secrecy that of all his ma[ties] councell only the Conde de Castel Mehor and the Secretary of State were acquainted with the business." As a matter of fact Sir Henry Bennet's letter of 25 July above referred to, informed Sir Richard that he was to be sent to Spain and that the Portugal Ambassador and the Spanish Agent O'Muledi had been informed of the decision, and it is clear it was intended that he should return to England first, as the Agent had demurred to the first English Ambassador to Spain after the Restoration, going to that Court by way of Lisbon.

Boswell Court, in which Lady Fanshawe took a house for two years on their return to England, lay under the n.w. angle of the site of the present Law Courts: nearly 80 years after her stay it was one of the many localities in London where Dr. Johnson lived, and shortly afterwards Fielding resided there also. Lady Fanshawe and her husband appear to have had a very busy time throughout September and October. Early in November he asked of the Lord Treasurer through Sir Philip Warwick, that he might receive £3000 for his equipage and £2000 for his transport to Spain and £400 *p.m.* for entertainment there—he also asked for an allowance for two Secretaries. On 20 November he obtained from the Lord Treasurer a warrant for payment of £1000 per quarter with effect from 1 September, though he had asked that the favour of its looking back might extend only to 12 September, when he waited on the King at Bath; but at the end of the month he could write to the Conde de Castel Melhor "mi embaxador per Madrid va avançando con passo Castellano" a saying which was to apply still more pertinently to his negotiations at the Spanish Court.* In a draft of 6 December addressed to the King of Portugal Sir Richard wrote that the King his master had complied with the request to send him as Ambassador to Madrid, retaining his old powers regarding Portugal as if residing there, and permitted him to communicate to the Portuguese Crown his instructions to Spain. In a note annexed to this the Ambassador

* It was apparently expected at Lisbon that Sir Richard would return there before proceeding to Spain, as Consul Maynard wrote on $\frac{18}{28}$ November (*State Papers Portugal, VI.*, 221) "it is impossible this Kingdom can long support the charges of this war without a considerable supply of money from other princes, and they hope that the Spaniards indigent condition will make them as inclinable to a peace as they are here."

urged that either Lyonell Fanshawe or Mr. Robert Crighton or Mr. John Price—all three, discreet faithfull and diligent and all completely lettered, one (Crighton) a M.A. of Cambridge, a fellow of Trinity College—might be recognised as his locum tenens at Lisbon. It may be recalled that the Lord Mayor, Sir John Robinson, with whom Sir Richard Fanshawe dined on 7 October, 1663, was grandfather of Sir John Robinson, fourth baronet, who married Mary Morgan, grand-daughter of Robert Sheffield and the Hon. Mary Fanshawe. Heylin's *Life of Laud* is dedicated to the Lord Mayor.

Sir Richard Fanshawe's instructions for his Spanish Embassy are dated 14 January, 1664, and on the same day the Lord Treasurer issued a pass to him to transport 12 horses, 2 coaches, 2 wagons, 1 litter and 100 trunks and cases from the kingdom (*Memoirs*, p. 219). The original of this was among the *Heathcote MSS.*, countersigned by the farmers of the customs, Jo. Wolstenholme, Jo. Jàcob, and J. Harrison, father of Lady Fanshawe. There is an independent account of the Ambassador's leaving London on 21 January after the rendezvous " in that half of the house " (Dorset House) " which Sr Thomas Fanshawe of Essex then lived in " as the text of the Memoirs should run, Mons. de Cominges* recording in a despatch of 4 February, 1664 (26 January O.S.) " Il y a quatre jours que M. Fanche est parti pour son ambassade d'Espagne dans un des plus superbes vaisseaux du Roi son maitre. Je crois que pour vanité il voulut passer devant ma porte (the French Ambassador was residing at Exeter House on the north side of the Strand nearly opposite Somerset House) afin que je visse son cortége qui l'accompagna jusqu' à son bord. Il etait dans une carosse du roi escorté de douse homme à cheval et suivi de vingt carosses a six chevaux. Il emmène un équippage de Jean de Paris,† sans parler de

* Gaston Jean Baptiste de Comenge or Comminges, Chenaye Des bois et Badier—one of the oldest families in Gascony.

† *Rugges Diurnal* of the date, specially notes that the Ambassador was accompanied by a noble retinue of noble Englishmen and household servants in a noble garbe. Such a following had

quantité des jeunes gentlehommes qui l'accompagnent pour curiosité Le Roi lui a fait donner en prêt seulement quatre tentures de fort belle tapisserie et quantité de vases et autre utensils en vermeil doré. Le peuple qui le suivait en foulet temoigna beaucoup de joie à son embarquement, et fit de grands vœux pour l'heureux succèss de la negotiation." From a letter of Sir Richard to Bennet of the date of 24 January, Portsmouth, it appears that he failed to find and take leave of the latter on the 21st, the Secretary of State having been called suddenly to Hampton Court.

When under sayle in Stokes Bay some days later (probably 31 January according to the statement in his subsequent letter from Torbay dated 13 February), the Ambassador addressed a letter to the King representing that Sir Edward Turnor, the Speaker, would move something to his Majesty on his behalfe (*Heathcote* MSS.) —The younger Sir Edward Turnor was born in 1643, according to the age recorded on the tomb of his wife, at Great Hallingbury, Essex (married in July, 1667, at St. Andrews, Holborn), and so was about 20 only when he went to Spain with Sir Richard: his father, Speaker and Chief Baron, is buried in the adjoining church of Great Parndon. Like Sir Richard, the younger Sir Edward and Sir Andrew King were made freemen of Portsmouth on 26 January. Sir Philip Honeywood was commander of the Portsmouth garrison only in 1664 —he became Lieutenant Governor two years later on the death of Sir William Berkeley and held that post till 1672.

Of the arrival of the Ambassador in Spain after a prosperous journey from Torbay of only 9 days, and of his reception there on $\frac{26 \text{ February}}{7 \text{ March}}$ and the journey to Madrid, Lady Fanshawe gives full details in the Memoirs, evidently based on some record which she had by her, but which does not appear among the *Heathcote*

its disadvantages and Bennet in a letter of 30 January (*Miscellanea Arlica*), notes that the sailing of the Fleet had been delayed by the unreadiness of some part of the Ambassador's train.

MSS. Indeed her account of the Spanish Embassy is much the most detailed part of her Memoirs and comprises one third of the whole; extracts from two of Maynard's letters may, however, be added here. In the first of these dated $\frac{11}{21}$ March, he says, "I may truly say his majesty has as many hearty prayers from the common people as their own King," and ending "Sir John Lawson passed by this place on the 2nd of March this stile with a fair wind, and in all probability my Lord Ambassador was landed at Cadiz three days after. Sir John was pleased to write me my Lord and his Lady and all his family were in good health" (*State Papers Portugal, VI.*, 251). In the other, dated 7 April, 1664 (VI., 259), Maynard wrote, "By letters which I received from Cadiz of the $\frac{6}{16}$ March my Lord Ambassador Fanshawe was received with very great demonstrations of joy in that place, and his entertainment was very noble, and there is order given to entertain his Excellency in all places where he lodges in his journey to Madrid at the King's charge." Lord Arlington, writing on 2 April, 1664 (*Miscellania Arlica*), notes, "we have no letter yet from Sir Richard Fanshawe in Spain, but all from thence assure us he hath much more than an extraordinary welcome."

Lord Sandwich traversed the same route, but from north to south, in 1668, and some interesting items of his journal are given here. He, too, found Don Diego de Ibara at Cadiz serving as Vice-Admiral* under the Duke of Veraguas, "a valiant soldier but no seaman at all," and recorded that de Ibara was the best seaman in Spain: a Spanish encomium of him ran "digno de mejor fortuna, caballero que procedié siempre con approbation valor y prudencia muy amado de las milicias por su

* The Earl noted previously in his diary, under November 20, 1667, that the Vice-Admiral had been removed and was living at Seville. He gives yet another variant of the name as de Ibarras. He also mentions that the Marquis of Trocifal (*Memoirs*, pp. 185, 189) was at Cadiz raising money to enable the fleet to go to sea. He himself was seriously indisposed there after his long journey in the great summer heat, and all the official visits paid to him were returned for him by Mr. Shirres. His journey from Xeres to Cadiz was made round by land and not by way of Port St. Mary.

agradevole cortesia." The Duke of Alburquerque had distinguished himself at sea in 1650 by defeating four French vessels bringing relief to Tortosa, in which year he succeeded Don Juan of Austria as General of the Galleys: he had previously distinguished himself at the battle of Rocroi in 1643 as a commander of cavalry. He died in 1676, twenty years before his wife.

Sending home a copy of the King's instructions for his reception in Spain, which expressly stated that "only for him this new thing is done"—Sir Richard wrote of the Duke of Medina Celi that he had received the honours prescribed both from the Duke "in his owne person and those of his son and daughter-in-law, the Duke and Duchesse of Alcala and Lerma (so they write themselves) . . . a matter of no small wonder to people of all degrees in Andalusia when they consider the ancient royalty of that house, with a new accesse of fortune in certaynty, and a fayre possibility besides by this match of his son . . . The truth is he appears as to parts, even of book learning, a man higher by the head than his fellows, being not only thought to know it himselfe, but to have most men of his opinion." But all the same Sir Richard was to have a persistent and bitter opponent in the Duke in all matters relating to Tangier, and facilities for English men-of-war. One of the letters to Spanish notables sent by the King of England with his Ambassador, was addressed to the Duke of Medina Celi. The bridge made at Port St. Mary to enable the Ambassador's party to land direct from the Royal barge was devised to take the place of the usual landing on the shoulders of Moorish porters, which is mentioned by various travellers and figured in the account of the *Voyages in Espagne*, par Mons. M., published in 1699, at Amsterdam. Colmenar remarks very truly of Port St. Mary, "Toute la baie est si bien decouverte qu'on peut voir Cadiz fort commodement du Port de S. Marie."

The cost of the Ambassador's journey from the sea to Madrid at the King's expense from 7 March to 30 April was so great that it was ordered that this

Don Ramiro Núñez de Guzmán, Duke of Medina de las Torres

Wikimedia Commons/University Library of Heidelberg

Lionel Fanshawe (1627–1687)

by John Michael Wright

Valence House Museum

should never be incurred again: the Spaniards might well have recalled Gongora's lines upon similar expenditure on the embassy of Lord Howard of Effingham, "But why make Luther rich and leave Spain poor." The Ambassadors of other States at the Court of Madrid of course resented the special honours accorded to Sir Richard, especially the French Ambassador, and announced their intention of claiming similar attentions in future. The Duke of Medina de las Torres suggested that the warmth of his welcome was due to the keen desire of the people of Andalusia for renewal of unrestricted commerce with England and the similarity of the English and Spanish natures, and in reporting this the Venetian Ambassador referred to the proverb, "Poter Spagna haver guerra con tutti, mai convenir pace con l'Inghilterra." In the *Heathcote MSS.* is a memo. recording that the gifts which Sir Richard gave to the Spanish domestics in Cadiz were £120 and in Seville £90, besides presents to the poor, and English prisoners. The Dukes of Medina Celi were Counts "de la cuidad e gran puerto de Santa Maria"—the seventh Duke became Captain General of the coasts of Andalusia in 1644, and in 1650 was thanked by letter issued by Milton, for his courtesies to Admiral Blake. Don Francisco Diaz de Baran y Benavides stands branded with the responsibility of the utter defeat of the Dutch and Spanish Fleets in Palermo harbour on 1 June, 1676, he having insisted that the latter should occupy the centre of the line.

At Seville Sir Richard no doubt met His Secretary Lyonell Fanshawe who had written to him from there on 7 and 16 March reporting that he had left Lisbon on 14 February, and arrived at Cadiz on the 17th, reaching Seville 5 days later, the Ambassador's property having been subjected to uncivil sniffing for civit amber or musk in it! Of the Assistente Don Pedro Conde de Molina de Herrera (whose brother Don Antonio Francisco Mesia de Tobar y Paz was Spanish Representative in England 1665-1669, and presented to

New College the beautiful grace cup still in possession of the College) Lord Sandwich noted, in his journal of his journey from Corunna to Madrid, when passing the town of El Castin (30 miles s.w. of Segovia), that the Conde was buried in a convent of nuns there, and that the family held the principal interest in the place, owning 20,000 sheep and 40,000 head of cattle. Of the Royal palace at Seville Lord Sandwich recorded "the king hath a very noble palace, anciently of the Moorish Kings but most magnificently and richly repaired by King Pedro el cruel and the Emperor Charles V, and of the most elaborate carved work that ever I saw." When Lady Fanshawe refused the Assistente's gift of a young lion, her husband might have quoted the Spanish proverb "no es segura compaña la del leon por manso que sea." A full account of the reception of the Ambassador at Seville appears in *Rugge's diurnal* of April, 1664.

Carmona is described by Lord Sandwich as on a hill a quarter of a mile perpendicular in height—on the day he was there, 28 July, he was 43 years of age: Ecija he praises as a fine town with many cavaliers of quality. At Cordova he stayed only one night and did not record any account of the place. The poet Gongora, who was a Cordovan by birth, writes of his mother-city (*Churton's translations*):—

"Ye lofty walls and Towers, exalted hold
Of Honour, Princely State and Knightly worth,
Where Guadalquiver like a King goes forth,
Of nobler name than streams with sands of gold;
And thou fair plain and stately mountains old
Which heaven indulgent hangs with wreaths of light;
My land for ever loved, in glory bright
The muses bower and nurse of warriors bold."

Lord Sandwich mentions the olives and oil production of Andujar, and the lead mines of Linares, the best in Spain, and that one of the now ruined forts at San Estaphan, as he terms it, was then in good repair and had a fine residence of the Benavides family in it. The great grandson of the Count, named by Lady Fanshawe, became Duke of San Esteban de Puerto in 1739. Lord Sandwich notes that the pass through the Sierra Morena between this place and Torre Juan Abad, was apt to be infested by robbers, and that the lord of the latter place was the poet Quevedo. Referring to the causeway over the depression of the Guadiana he notes that many tortoises were caught in that. [In April, 1905, I saw a very large brown snake coiled up on the bank in front of one of the piers of the long bridge.] Of Consuegra he records that the town and the villages round it, once belonging to Roderick the Goth, were held by the Prior of San Juan (at that time Don Juan of Austria and of Mora), and that it then produced as much wine as any place in La Mancha, though it is nowadays entirely out-distanced by Manzernares. At Toledo also Lord Sandwich remained only one night—there could be no sufficient reason for lingering in a journey through the heart of Spain in midsummer—and stayed with a silk merchant: Calmenor gives an excellent account of this city, as of Cordova. At Getafe his first stage out of Madrid lying s.w. of Sir Richard's last halting place Vallecas, he saw large numbers of tinajas in cuevas (cellars) as Lady Fanshawe had seen at Esquivias, and notes that the amount of fuller's earth used to clear the wine was 1 lb. to every 10 arrobas (32 pints). A large tinaja may be seen in the London Guildhall Museum.

The Fanshawes came to a house in Madrid outside the Fuencarral Gate in the St. Barbara Quarter, on 8 June, and Sir Richard's public reception took place on Wednesday the 18th of that month. The fille-morte brocade of his splendid court dress is illustrated by his line in the translation of the *Pastor Fido* (Act I., Scene v.):—

> "How ye make
> Pale feulemort a pure vermillion take."

A portrait of Sir Richard Fanshawe which is of remarkable merit is reproduced at p. 160. The god Alpheus will be seen in the background emerging from the river Alpheo, as he appears in the frontispiece of the 2nd edition (1648) of Sir Richard's translation of Guarini's *Pastor Fido.* The mask, representing the Drama, is introduced at the foot of the picture.

The compliment of the French Ambassador, Georges d'Aubusson, Archbishop of Embrun, in sending his coach to accompany the British Representative to court was, as noted at p. 501 of the *Memoirs*, a double-edged one connected with the French claim of precedence, and it is on record that when the Venetian Ambassador was received at Court on 19 September and the coach of the English Ambassador was expected to escort him, the "fiery" Archbishop of Embrun sent a large number of armed men with his cortege to maintain his precedence which he had been ordered to assert at any cost. The fact of his doing so is attested by an independent witness, Count Poetting; and it is stated by Fornier in his *Histoire des Alpes maritimes*, that to provide against the contingency of any claim to precedence by the English Ambassador a number of the Gardes du Corps were sent to Madrid as gentlemen of the household of the Archbishop.* The English King's order that other Ambassadors' coaches were not to attend the public entry of an Ambassador (*Heathcote* MSS., p. 83) therefore

* As early as $\frac{18}{28}$ January, 1664, Comminges had recommended Embrum should be informed of Fanshawe's coming, and be warned to be upon his guard "ces gens cy ne pretendant en aucune nous ceder la premire place." The Archbishop declared openly to the Venetian Ambassador that the order of the King of Spain, that no coaches were to accompany the English Ambassador on the occasion of his public reception on 18 June, was solely aimed at his claim to precedence, and that he had advised the French court to refuse to submit to it. And indeed in the letter of de Lyonne of 16 October, referred to in the text as giving details of the steps taken by Embrum to protect his cortege, it is stated that 2 days before the State reception of the Venetian Ambassador, the order regarding the accompaniment of coaches was withdrawn, and that the English Ambassador had 2 coaches ready to send, one placed well down the route and intended to take place of the French Ambassador's by the force of a hundred English and Portuguese secretly entertained by him and fifty Venetian bandoliers, who were however deterred by the arrangements and bold front of the French, and Comminges wrote on the same date to de Lionne that he had news that there had been "quelque demesle" between the two Ambassadors on this occasion and that the English attempt had failed. So was political history made in the XVII. century!

Catherine of Braganza arriving at Portsmouth, 1662

LBBD Archives, Valence House

Present-day photograph of Casa de las Siete Chimeneas, Madrid (House of the Seven Chimneys)

Wikimedia Commons

saved Sir Richard from being exposed to such a struggle as occurred between the entourages of the Comte d'Estrades and the Baron Batteville on Tower Hill on 10 October, 1661.

Of the companions of Sir Richard on the occasion of his public reception full notes have been given at pp. 478-80 and 502-5 of the *Memoirs*. Of Sir Andrew King it may be further noted that his father came to London from Bishop's Castle in Shropshire; and that both of them were freemen of the Merchant Tailors' Co., Sir Andrew being apprenticed in 1606 and admitted in 1613; and being subsequently married to the widow of his master Mr. John Sharowe; after which he resided at Ankerwyke House. He must have been a very old man when he died in 1678. Sir Benjamin Wright was connected by marriage with Sir Richard Fanshawe, his mother being the sister of Sir Oliver Boteler of Sharnbrook and Teston, and therefore aunt of Sir William Boteler the first husband of Sir Richard's sister Joan. Full details of the Wright family are recorded in the *Essex Visitation* of 1634, in which Sir Benjamin is entered as being in Spain: it is on record that he was so in Lord Aston's time (1636), and he may have been known then to Sir Richard. He was mentioned by Lord Sandwich as late as 1667, but the date of his death is not known.

The delay in providing a suitable residence for the English Ambassador in Madrid was not due, for once, to Spanish supineness. The order reserving it for him was dated 11 June (it being noted that the Siete Chimeneas House was the residence "en che han venido todos los embaxadores de Ynglaterra") three days after Sir Richard came into the capital and seven days before the successor of the Venetian Ambassador arrived (on the very date of the public reception of the English Ambassador), and therefore no doubt the English Representative had a prior right to the house which the Court had secured for him by order. But with the object of defeating this, the new Italian Legate came into the house secretly while his predecessor was still there, and then set up a claim of continuous possession. It was, of course, impossible for the Spanish Court to submit to this defiance of its prerogative, and though Sir Richard was not unwilling to waive his prior right, the Duke of Medina de las Torres refused to allow this to be done, alleging that his master's honour was closely affected by the point in dispute and that his order in his own capital must be obeyed.

We find Comminges recording on 10 July, 1664, "Le temps qui meurit toutes choses m'a justifié aupres du Chancelier Heyden (Hyde), et s'il m'a cru effectivement espagnol, je serai présentement selon son gout. Il magnifie avec de belles paroles le bon acceuil que l'on fait au Sieur Fanshau à Madrid, l'amitié particuliere de M. le Duc de las Torres, et l'estime de toute la nation, et la courtesie de M. de Batteville qui l'a voulu contraindre à prendre son logis."

The agreement for the lease of the house was executed on 11 July, 1664, by Don Antonio Suarez de Melo, and was witnessed by Don Benjamin Ruit and Don Leonel Fanshawe. On 13 August Sir Andrew King sent home a long account of the dispute "for that it hath caused discourse." The Venetian Ambassador finally gave way, he reports, on 6 August (*State Papers Spain, Bundle* 46). The Ambassador referred to, who was obliged by the Court to leave the house, was Marin II. Zorzi di Marino, who succeeded Giorgio Cornaro* (a direct descendant of the brother of Caterina Cornaro

* Corner, who had reported the special honours paid to the English Ambassador on arriving in Spain and journeying to Madrid, informed the Venetian Government that he was a person well thought of in Spain where he had been Secretary to (Lord) Bristol, and that though he was a gentleman by birth he was of merchant descent, and in consequence had been made qualified for his present post by the title of milord and by being made a member of the Council of State (much of which was of course incorrect). By the special kindness of Mr. Horatio Brown and the Director of the State Archives, Venice, it has been possible to obtain various extracts from the despatches of the Venetian Ambassador during the years 1664-66. These however are reported to be generally in a terribly decayed condition though it has been possible to make copies of a full narrative of the deaths of King Philip IV. and Sir Richard Fanshawe, as will appear below.

Queen of Cypres), in June, 1664, and after being Ambassador at Vienna and holding other high offices, died as Capitano a Padova in 1675. *The Venetian State records* show that the Signoria strongly backed their representative at Madrid, and that a residence acceptable to him was not provided till October, 1664: both he and his predecessor were very much younger than Sir Richard Fanshawe.

No doubt the decision of the Court that the Siete Chimeneas House should pass to the English Ambassador on its being vacated by the Venetian Legate was very galling to the State, especially as the Secretary of their succeeding Ambassador and his belongings were already in the house. Fortunately the good sense of their representative prevailed (in spite of the evil advice of the Archbishop of Ebrun of whose discussion with the two Ambassadors a very lengthy account is given in their letter of 22 June to the Serenissimo Principe, the Doge), his conclusion being "che il pontiglio di una casa non deve prejiudicare il servitio publico," and it was arranged that his possession of the house should be recognised on his promise to vacate it after a few days; and in their letter of 11 October the Venetian authorities rightly commended Marin 2nd Zorzi di Marino for the settlement effected by him, "risultando tutto in decoro della Signoria nostra et in augmento di posto alla Vostra Rappresentanza." The Baron de Batteville was used as an intermediary in the case, and informed Cornaro that Sir Richard was vexed by the statement that he had demanded the house, which had been offered to him without any action on his part, and was willing to stay on in his present residence. It is to be regretted therefore that further trouble arose in connection with the first visit between the two representatives of the West and East at the Spanish Court.

Cornaro had not paid a visit to Sir Richard after his public reception, his excuse being partly that he was suffering from dysentery, but really that he had taken leave of the Court and was therefore no longer accredited

Ambassador on 18 June,* having had his farewell audience on $\frac{11}{21}$ May; and Sir Richard in consequence declined to call on Zorzi after his public reception, which seems unlike his usual line of considerate courtesy, especially as he had sent his gentleman to convey his compliments to Cornaro. The Venetian State wisely urged that the difference should also be made up, and suggested that their Representative should call on the English Ambassador's wife first "che intendemo trovasi costi, et que (la visita) non admette formalita cospicue et uguali a quelle del marito." This apparently he did not do, as Lady Fanshawe makes no mention of any civilities on his part. But neither does she do so as regards the French Ambassador, who was the inveterate opponent of the English policy at the Court of Spain from first to last as St. Roman was at Lisbon, as will be seen below. Sir Richard reported, however, on the $\frac{10}{20}$ November, 1664, that the French Ambassador had now paid him a second visit after three months, "frequent visits not being usual in this court"; and in a letter of 23 November Sir Richard refers to a return visit of his on the 22nd to the French Ambassador, and of an argument of the latter with the Dutch Ambassador upon which Sir Richard slyly suggested that the Cardinal's hat which he might reasonably expect in reward for his present embassy should be transferred from him to the Dutch Ambassador, at which his French Excellency "laughed very well again." We also know of another visit 14 months later (January, 1664) from the latter, just before Sir Richard started for Portugal.

By a slip, the sentence on p. 153 of the *Memoirs* which should run: "The Duke de Medina de las Torres having procured a letter here from *the Pope's Nuntio to give me leave to see* the convent there" (the Escorial), was printed with the omission of the words italicised to the confusion of the meaning of the sentence.† Lady

* See *Fanshawe letters*, 1702, pp. 81, 129, 185.

† The Nuntio at Madrid in October, 1664, was Cardinal Caroli Bonelli, titular Archbishop of Corinth, created Cardinal in January of that year. He was succeeded in December by Vitelliano Visconti,

Fanshawe's description of the Escorial is taken from the work of de los Santos, who correctly states that the great stones forming the sides of the principal entrance were 24 feet high, not 12 as mistakenly recorded in the *Memoirs*, this dimension being the breadth of the portal; and that each of these great jambs had to be conveyed to the site in " a fortissimo carro que tiravam quaranta pares de Bueyes "—40 yoke of Oxen. Los Santos gives high praise to the painting of the battle of Lepanto by Canxisso (Luca Cambisso) and to a number of pictures by this artist at the Escorial. Gongora wrote one sonnet on the battle and another on the Convent and Palace.

The Casa del Campo Aranjuez, and the Escorial which Sir Richard and Lady Fanshawe visited in October 1664, are specially mentioned by Lord Sandwich in his *Diary*. An excellent brief description of the last is given by James Howell (d. 1666).

While the controversy regarding the House he was to occupy was going on, and before he was established in that which was eventually accorded to him, Sir Richard, writing to his " Right Honorable and very singular Good Lord," the Lord Treasurer, on 29 July, 1664 (Fanshawe Letters, p. 168), thanked him for his " most Noble and singular Care, in ordering effectual Supplies " to the Spanish embassy, adding that he assured his Lordship in reference to the King " that I will once more take upon me the Title of his Majestiess *Remembrancer of his Revenues*, so far as faithfully to advertise your Lordship, whenever I shall plainly find that all the service that can be farther done his Majesty in this Court, will not be worth the cost of an Ambassador

titular Archbishop of Ephesus, created Cardinal in February, 1666, and made Archbishop of Monreale in Sicily by the Spanish Crown in 1668, when he was followed, as noted by Lord Sandwich, by Frederigo Borromeo, who became Cardinal in 1670. He was titular Patriarch of Alexandria, so the three Nuntios may be said to have spanned between them the whole of the east coast of the Mediterranean. The *Vatican records* naturally contain very little regarding the English Ambassador, but the special orders for his entertainment on his arrival at Cadiz and journey to Madrid and the action of the French Ambassador on the occasion of the public reception on 18 June, are duly noted.

here." This, and probably other letters in the same tone, led Sir Philip Warwick on 21 October (*Fanshawe Letters*, p. 350), to write to his brother in law that the little progress made in his negotiations was attributed at home to the difficulty of his proposals and the dilatory Genius of the Spaniards, and that if they wanted only so formal a treaty as the old one the two nations could be "of no great Consideration to one another, not any such as you and I were wont to wish in the *Pall-mall*; and I am sure not such as you would have trode that Stage for; yet, since you are upon the Place, learn the Humour of the Nation with patience, and let no heat of yours, but positive and distinct Orders from your Superiours make you affect your return"—a very wise and kindly epistle, ending "My Wife prays for you, and all those that have outgrown the name of little Ones."

No doubt the victory of Montes Claros (which took place on the 17 June, 1665) tended to stiffen the attitude of the Portuguese, and the Jesuit intrigues at the front, and those of the Marquis de Liche at Lisbon (according to d'Ablancourt), added to the determination not to treat with Spain unless the title of King were conceded. But all the same Sir Richard Fanshawe seems to have had grounds for believing that his original proposals might be accepted, as Consul Maynard wrote to Lord Arlington on $\frac{8}{18}$ February, following the very time of the Ambassador's arrival at Benevente, "I never saw a greater alteration in so short a space as I have seen within this fortnight in the common people of this city, who then cried nothing but for peace, and nothing else could satisfy them, and now they are altogether for war, saying that the conditions now proferred will ruin them and strange expressions are thrown out against my Lord Fanshaw," a result partly due no doubt to the above intrigues, but mainly to French intervention and French gold.

The health of the King of Spain was causing grave anxiety in 1665. The Nuntio Visconti sent detailed reports of his increasing illness in that summer: on the occasion of the Nuntio's last visit to him on 26 August the King was obliged to keep his seat while he received him. The State papers contain a very full account of the death and burial of Philip IV. which perhaps Lady Fanshawe had before her when she wrote her Memoirs, though she does not follow it quite exactly. The King was taken dangerously ill on Friday, 11 September, received the viaticum on the 14th, and supreme unction and the papal benediction by the Nuntio on the 15th, took leave of the Queen and her son and daughter and died on Thursday, 17th, his death being announced by the order to the German Guard to proceed to the quarter of the King, Charles II. The coffin of Philip IV, remained closed, with the crown and sceptre on two cushions lying upon it, until the Grand Funeral mass began; it was then unlocked by the oldest of the Major Domos, the Count of Puebla de la Mont Albano, and the crown and sceptre were thereupon held by two of the noble guard at the foot of the platform on which the coffin rested. The cross held by the dead man was of gold and contained a fragment of the cross. The description given of the dress is "panno plateado richissimo d'argento," of the stockings, "à color di perle," and of the boots, of black chamois-leather—the suit being that in which the King was married to his second wife. The Patriarch of the Indies, who had performed the deathbed ministrations, accompanied the dead King to his burial.*

Sir Richard Fanshawe's new credentials were sent to him on 23 October, 1665 (*Harleian*, 7010, f. 418), and were received by him long before $\frac{5}{15}$ December. Unluckily, he was persuaded by the Duke de Medina de las Torres to hold them back, and he did not present them to the Queen till $\frac{12}{22}$ December, as reported in his letter of $\frac{13}{23}$ December to Lord Arlington (*Harleian*, 7010, f. 464). In the letter forwarding them, Lord Arlington

* Wiquefort asserts that the power of an Ambassador ceases when the Prince who employs him, or he to whom he is employed, is no longer in a condition to act, that is to say, by the death of either.

wrote, "we shall this week bring together the Spanish Ambassador and the Lords Commissioners to treat about public articles of peace with that crown and take for our ground work the old printed articles together with what was transacted between the Duke of Medina de las Torres and yourself last year at Madrid. Upon all which I pray you let us have your newer thoughts, if you have any, by the next." Lord Arlington's letter of 10 December gave intimation of the appointments of Lord Sandwich and Sir Robert Southwell, and another of 17 December, from Oxford, formally announced the resolution of sending Lord Sandwich as Extra Ambassador and directed Sir Richard to hold his hand till Lord Sandwich's arrival, declaring the reason and assuring the Spaniards that Lord Sandwich would carry with him "a full and entire satisfaction to all their wishes." Three days later the appointment of Sir R. Southwell to Lisbon was announced from the same place, and on 7 January Arlington stated that Sir R. Southwell was leaving England the next day, and Lord Sandwich would be despatched the following week (*Harleian* 7010, f. 473).

Lady Fanshawe gives but very brief indications in the *Memoirs* of her husband's mid-winter journey to Portugal which kept him absent from Madrid from 16 January, 1666 to 8 March. This was undertaken in accordance with his original instructions of 14 January, 1664 (*Fanshawe Letters*, p. 19), that ran—"In case they shall consent to enter into a Treaty of Peace or Truce with the Kingdom of *Portugal* by our Mediation, you shall, by giving advertisement thereof to that King by such Messenger as you shall send thither, and according to the powers you have from us, qualifie him as the occasion shall require, by vertue of that Letter of Credence which you have to the said King for the said effect. And the Treaty of Peace or Truce having further progress, you shall offer to transport yourself to the Frontier, or to *Lisbon*, there in Person to perform such farther Offices therein as shall be requisite, giving us constant and punctual Advertisement of all your Proceedings, that you may be furnished from hence with any new Powers and Instructions you have need of." Among the *Heathcote* MSS.* are both a programme of his route westward, and a memo. of his actual journey to and fro; and in the Journals of Lord Sandwich was happily found a full account of the travels given to Mr. Godolphin by Mr. Parry, who accompanied the Ambassador with his ward, a son of Mr. John Ashburnham.

On 4 January, 1666, 12 days before leaving Madrid for Portugal, Sir Richard reported that the Duke of Medina de las Torres had told him that the French Ambassador declared that the King of France had resolved to break with England and demanded free use of the Spanish ports for the Duke of Beaufort's Fleet of forty sayle, and had protested against the league defensive and offensive, which he asserted had, according to his certain knowledge, been concluded between Spain and England. (*Harleian* 7010, f. 485.)

From the *Journals of the Earl of Sandwich* the following notes are taken:—

On 16 January the Ambassador left Madrid and lay at Illescas, and on the 17th at Toledo, where he was met with many good words and prayers, the city being half ruined by the cessation of its trade with Portugal; on the 18th he was at Mora, on the 19th at Malagon and on the 20th at Conral de Calatrava. On the 21st he stayed at Saceruela, the last town of La Mancha, and on the 22nd at Tallarubias, the first town of Estramadura, where he met Spanish horse proceeding to Catalonia on the strength of the expected treaty with Portugal. On the 23rd he was entertained by the Governor at Villa Nueva de la Serena, and on the 24th halted at Oliva (de Merida, belonging to the order of St. Iago), pushing forward early on the 25th to Zafra, where he had been told the Marquis

* The Editor of the *Heathcote MSS.*, Mrs. Lomas, to whom the present writer was much indebted for many kindnesses, in his editing Lady Fanshawe's Memoirs, naturally omitted from the papers of these *MSS.* chosen for publication a number which, though of no general public value, are of great family interest regarding Sir Richard Fanshawe and his wife

of Caracena, the Spanish General, had been ordered by the Queen to meet him. The General's Spanish pride or sloth, however, prevented his being there first, and the Ambassador went on to Medina de las Torres, where his friend the Duke "hath the dominion of two decayed Towers for a testimony" of his title. On the 27th the party arrived at Frejenal where he was magnificently entertained, and waited a day for the return of his Second Secretary, Mr. John Price, who had passed through that place on his return from Portugal to Aracena. Learning that his route from here was practicable only for saddle mules, the Ambassador changed his plans and proceeded on the 29th to Encinasola the last Spanish town and on the 30th crossed the Raya and travelling all day through mountains, came late to Santele Jo (San Alexo), where he was met with all imaginable expressions of joy and goodwill. On 31 January he was welcomed by Count Schomberg, General of all the strangers, and conducted to Moura; on 1 February he crossed the Guadiana and moved on to Vidigueira (belonging to the Marquis of Nizza, formerly Conde de Vidigueira), and on the 2nd came to Viana where he was entertained by the Count and where many of the English officers met him. On the 3rd he was received at Evora by the Conde de Vimiosa, and passing through Montemoro (Novo) and Coruche came on 6 February to Benavente,* "a little

* Benavente is on the Raia some 5 miles east of the point where that river suddenly turns North and falls into the Tagus, Salvatierra (which should be Salvaterra), lies 6 miles north of Benevente and 3 miles south of the latter stream. A week before he arrived the Queen mother of Portugal died at the convent of Xabrejas in Lisbon. It is curious that there should be no mention of this in the records of the conferences at Benevente. In the translation of the *Memoirs of Mons. Ablancourt* it is noted of this time, "Every one was taken up at Lisbon with the propositions of peace which were made by my lord Fanchon, with preparations for the reception of the Princess of Nemours, and the death of the Queen mother." The French representative recorded an honourable epitaph of her that "During her Regency she had omitted nothing for the defence of the State; and after she had delivered herself from the snares of her enemies, she supported with a great deal of courage and resolution her retreat or rather her prison."

village nigh a league from Salvatierra,* whither the King comes in January staying till Lent for hunting's sake. Here was a house well furnished for his Exc^y^., and his camarades and Gentlemen had each a very good lodging provided in the houses; his Exc^y^. had seven meales, and those very sumptuous ones from the King, and the use of the King's linen and plate and other necessaries for his house all the time he stay'd." The rest of Mr. Parry's narrative of what occurred during the stay at Benevente is of sufficient interest and importance for quotation in full.

"Here his Exc^y^. according to what he heard from Madrid a few days before found Sir Robert Southwell, who was sent as envoy for the making of this, as 'twas thought already concluded, agreement. He landed at Lisbone on 20th Jan^y^., the court being then at Salvatiera. Antonio de Souza Sec^y^ of State presently entertained him with a long relation of what had passed between the Jesuit at Badajos, Caracena's confessor, on the one side, and the Rector of Elvas on the other, making the whole transaction amount unto this as if Spayne had promised powers in that overture to treat from king to king; but said he would put an immediate stop to that proceeding

* Sir R. Southwell sailed from Portsmouth on Saturday, 6 January, 1666, and reached Cascaes Bay on Tuesday the 16th, but was not allowed to land till the evening of the 18th, after demonstrating the freedom of his party from plague by springing out their arms and legs cutting capers and drumming on their bellies! (Letter of $\frac{\text{22 Jan.}}{\text{1 Feb.}}$ *Addl MSS.*, 34, 366, f. 24.) He then learnt for the first time that Sir Richard Fanshawe was on his way to Portugal "with no ordinary hopes of a good conclusion," and had decided to go up the river that night to Salvaterra, so as to leave the newly arrived French Envoy no advantage of time. Accordingly he arrived there on 2 February and had a long interview with the Conde de Castel Melhor, and another at Benevente on the 3rd. On $\frac{\text{Jan. 25}}{\text{Feb. 4}}$ he reported to Lord Arlington that the Conde flatly demanded their title and a peace, and if Spain proposed anything in consideration thereof, be it so and they would here consider of it. His Excellency took occasion to tell me that Sir Richard Fanshawe was suddenly expected here to impart somewhat on this subject, of which I told him I knew nothing before my arrival and that I believed some letters to him from England have had misfortune in France, or else he might probably have continued at Madrid till my arrival there," a statement hardly likely to strengthen the authority of the English Ambassador in the negotiation for which he was coming from Spain.

because Sir Richard Fanshawe just in that nick wrote to me he was coming and that he brought with him what he believed would be to their satisfaction, and concluded that the title of King was obtayned by him, it happening so in the nick with the other overture. So that hereupon Sir Robert hastening up to the court, because the French envoy was just then arrived and was gone thither, and arriving there on 2nd Feby. being Tuesday, he found that all his sollicitations were to no effect, and that they would yield nothing to him because they believed Sir Richard Fanshawe was bringing all they desired—who arrived at Benavente, as was said before, on Saturday the 6th of February. Sunday Feby 7th the Conde de Castel Melhor came to visit His Excy the Ld Ambassador to whom after a long discourse the Ambassador delivered his treaty; which the Conde carrying with him to court to peruse after a little reading found the title of King wanting, which put them all into a high mutiny, and the Conde sent it back again that very night without reading further than the commission, where the Government of Portugal was mentioned; and the first message after this that the Lord Fanshawe had was on Tuesday by Antonio de Souza now at court, telling him that the councell had passed an order to persuade his Excy not to desire audience. However he received frequent visites from the Grandees and severall particular civilities.

"During this time Sir Robert Southwell was not acquainted with the treaty, but on Wednesday morning (10th) was spoke to by Sir Richard Fanshawe, and the whole being then communicated, how he obtained at Madrid a truce for 30 years,* that they were called the present Government of Portugall, that prisoners should be of either side released, that the towns should remain in the hands of the possessors etc. But all being refused in Portugall unless they were treated with as King and had a peace, His Excy asked Sir Robert Southwell whether he would join him in this proposal, viz., that supposing the Queen of Spayne would immediately issue a commission empowering fulano (such a one) to treat as with the

King of Portugall and for a peace to be made, whether the Portuguese would on this condition and in view of the said commission forthwith ratify the present treaty, that so the articles of it might take immediate effect for the cessation of arms. Sir Robert Southwell consented hereto, Sir Richard making the proposition and engaging to send to Madrid about it, and Sir Robert promising the ratification of his Matie of England if both parties here should concur therein.

" But this overture was flatly denied with signification from the Conde de Castel Melhor that his Master by the advice of his councell had resolved never to treat of anything with Spayne untill Spayne first agreed to treat with him as from King to King. At this pause the matter stood for some days, whilst Feby 12th Sir Robert had publique audience of the King. Afterwards Sir Robert showing the Conde de Castel Melhor how impossible it was to bring the Spaniard to such an agreement, where they should yield up all that was fought for by pronouncing the title of King and not to be assured at the same time to have any consideration for him, not so much as a promise that prisoners should be released; and therefore Sir Robert told him it was not proper to christen the child before it was borne, or not to lay down certain material points and articles of apparent benefitt to Spayne in case Spayne should comply with what they desired, and therefore it was most proper to set down the material points together with the formal ones.

" To this he answered that it was so reasonable that he would move that day in Councell that the first order should be changed; and accordingly [he wrote] (the next day) that Sir Richard Fanshawe and Sir Robert should give him a meeting, which accordingly they did at a convent [at Jerico] in the midway between the Court and Benavente; and there the Conde explained to them the points which they demanded, viz., the title of King and a peace, for which they would give all the prisoners immediate liberty, the Portuguese [refugees in Spain] their estates, but within certain limitation, etc., which points he advised we should draw up in such forme as they might be presented them for an answer, whereupon which they would sygne unto and fix in. The Lord Ambassador and Sir Robert accordingly drew up the matter, but not to that extent to their favour as they desired; which when they came to reply unto they excepted against the shortness of some of the articles and explaining to what extent they would have them exprest, they signed and sealed the whole as appears by the projèct. With this being at that time the utmost the Portuguese would be brought unto, the Lord Ambassador and Sir Robert Southwell on Feby 22nd, set out from Benavente towards Madrid."

This account is entirely borne out by Sir Robert Southwell's letters to Lord Arlington, *Addl. MSS.*, 34, 338 British Museum. Sir Robert explains that it was agreed between him and Sir Richard that in the first instance the latter should proceed in his negotiations alone, so that if they failed Sir Robert might come in with his proposals from England. He adds that when he returned from his audience with the King (to which he was accompanied by Sir Richard's gentlemen and train,) and at which he delivered letters to the King, who spoke of his affection to his brother of England, and of his passion for the Queen his sister, and to Dom Pedro, and they found how flat the answer to their proposal was, Sir Richard wrote to the Conde de Castel Melhor that he intended to return to Madrid in 2 days; and that it was upon receipt of this that the Conde suddenly proposed the meeting at the Jerico convent. When they came to an understanding there the Conde promised that Portugal would hearken to England and embrace its interests and not give ear to France "giveing my Lord Ambassador many words of value and respect, as indeed his candour in proceeding and his labours in this businesse doe justly deserve."

And so the long journey back to Madrid was commenced, the first two stages being to Coruche also on the Raia, and Pavia, and the 24 and 25 February being spent at Estremoroz and Elvas, the Governor of the latter place sending the keys of the town to Sir Richard for the night, by way of compliment as at Cadiz in March, 1664. On the 26th the Spanish frontier and the Cayajo stream were passed, and after a mid-day meal at Badajoz to which Sir Richard proceeded from the boundry in the Governor's coach, the night was spent at Talavera la Real. On the 27th Merida was reached with its Triumphal arch, and ruined amphitheatre, and on the 28th, Medellin with a fine modern bridge across the Guadiana. The following stages were: March 1, Truxillo, 2nd, Jaraisejo, 3rd, Naval Moral, with a splendid bridge of two arches over the Tagus, and 4th, Oropesa, from which Sir Richard sent his last letter to his wife having sent two previous letters from Coruche and Medellin. Thence the route lay through, 5th, Talavera de la Reyna, 6th, Sant Ollala, 7th, Casa Rubias, where father Patrick,* confessor of the Duke of Medina de las Torres, met Sir Richard; and on the 8th, leaving Sir Robert Southwell at Mosteles to come into Madrid by litter at night, he being still incognito to the Spanish Court, the Ambassador, quitting the Duke's coach for his own on meeting "his lady and his 3 eldest daughters," arrived at his own house again.†

What happened thereupon diplomatically may also be told in the words of Mr. Parry and Sir Robert Southwell, Lady Fanshawe's narrative in the Memoirs being naturally very bare and brief. It must be remembered that the Spanish Court had been for nearly two months in possession of the news that Lord Sandwich was coming to it as Ambassador Extraordinary; and for

* Father Patrick O'Duffy, an Irish Franciscan, whom Sir Richard mentioned in his letter of 4 November, 1664 (*Fanshawe Letters*, p. 304), as lately returned from Rome with a new title of Defender of his Order, a place (as I am told) of great Eminence.

† The return route of Sir Richard was followed by Lord Sandwich in his journey from Madrid to Lisbon, 26 December, 1667—11 January, 1668, as far as Estromoz, whence he went direct to Lisbon through Montemor and Aldea Gallega on the south bank of the Tagus. Coming back between 6 and 22 March, 1668, Lord Sandwich took the same way as far as Talavera de la Reyna, whence he proceeded to Madrid via Toledo and Aranjuez.

a shorter time, of the news that the King of England would not ratify the treaty of 17 December as it stood; and that this not only disabled Sir Richard to a great extent in his efforts to promote the peace, but gave them a really solid reason for delay (to which the Spanish Council was always prone, having no decided policy of its own) until his successor should arrive, especially as the Conde de Molina had been informed in London that Lord Sandwich would bring proposals which would satisfy them in every way. Sir Robert's account contained in a letter of 30 March to Lord Sandwich (*State papers Spain* 50, p. 65) is as follows:—"We arrived here on the 8th instant where presenting* the said proposals and desiring Audience we found this court highly inflamed at the said demands, declaring that the King of England was bound to force Portugal to accept the proposals carried thither, or to turn his arms against them, at least to withdraw himself from their aid, and untill they heard whether the King did not hold himself obliged to ratify that treaty or what answer he would make on the refusal there of Portugal, they would not at all discourse with us on that point." Mr. Parry says roundly that the projèct when taken to the Queen and seen in Council was immediately sent back in imitation of the proceedings of Portugal, and Sir Robert was refused an audience unless he had somewhat to say in other affairs. So the matter stood till 24 March, though a reply was due to Portugal by the end of the month, when Sir Robert intimated that he should leave the next day unless the Queen positively commanded him to the contrary, and in consequence received a very gracious audience on the 25th, "after a thousand minds in these ministers whether or how he should be admitted" (Sir R. Fanshawe's letter of that date *Harleian* 7010 fo. 485), being introduced by Sir Richard Fanshawe (Letter of Sir Robert Southwell 30 March, 1666—*State Papers Spain* 50, p. 65), who

* This was on 12 March—to the Duke of Medina de las Torres—*Harleian* 7010, 147.

at the same time delivered into the hands of the Queen "a full justification* of all his proceedings" (Parry), which made it "evident (Southwell) that the Court here was by somebody strangely misinformed to think the King of England was bound to oblige Portugal to accept the conditions sent, or that he wd. ratify any articles till they were agreed on either side, and that being only Mediator not Arbitrator he could but persuade not bind till both parties thought fit." In this letter to Lord Sandwich Sir Robert Southwell gives a very clear and able summary of the situation.

"The present impediments of our business are first the natural, and now for want of a Minister, the accidental slowness in proceeding to any resolution here, next their aversion to yield to what Portugal does demand, and declaring their incapacity to do it by reason of the minority of the King. next their not suffering us (more than we do it by particular applications) to persuade them of the necessity of the thing and how little the point in difference is, for the Portuguese do not insist on any abjuring of the title or renouncing it by an Article to them, but merely to have it by way of appellation in the preface of the treaty. next they think that they shall hear by your Excellency that the King our master does acknowledge himself bound to them (as against the Portuguese) by

* The original of these is in the *Siamancas Records*. The paper was a very long one and not very well shaped for the purpose of submission to the council to which of course the Queen had to send it, and it is not necessary to quote at length from it here. In his letter of 16/26 March to Lord Arlington (*Harleian* 7010, 485) Sir Richard wrote that some days before Don Pedro Fenandez del Campo, being the most violent of the ministers who asserted the view in question, came to him and urged that "the King our master was obliged even to force a consent from the King of Portugal to the articles I carried thither only upon tryal . . . The which I very highly resenting on my own behalf . . . have this day put into the hands of her Majesty a memorial infallibly demonstrating to the contrary and further acquainting her Majesty with my late received orders (having first tried all other ways in vain) to endeavour in his Majesty's name to the utmost with this Court a peace in the form now insisted upon with Portugal from which might be easily gathered what his Majesty's resolution will be upon the declyning that Adjustment which I carried." The end of the memorial merely desired that the Ambassador "con vuestra magestad no pierda el credito de hombre de su palabra."

the treaty made hére, tho' my Lord Ambassador has made the contrary so palpable to them. And lastly that if your Excellency shall press them (as we do) to yield the title and a peace, since no mitigation of it can be had in Portugal, yet they will first expect to hear how if the King does not resent the denial of the Portuguese and the demands they make, of which we acknowledge to them we gave the King an account from Portugal, and although I tell them my instructions did suppose all these cases would happen, and how accordingly I should act when they did, and repeating again and again the great danger of letting this month pass without a resolution for the so long Portugal had bound itself up from the French, but would after be at liberty to do as they list, yet nothing can charm them they will do their own business their own way." On $\frac{11}{21}$ April Lord Sandwich replied to Sir Robert summarising the state of affairs as he understood them (*Harleian MSS.* 7010, f. 507) and concluding thus, "You may therefore as from me undeceive (the Spanish Ministers) from expecting any mitigation by my coming, and show my earnest desire that they would concede this point which is the Topstone that finisheth all, and I think most to their own and the general benefit; and press for a very speedy answer, that you may forthwith return into Portugal and perfect this affair.

"But now if Spain (notwithstanding they know I can give them no ease in this matter) shall find reason to run all the hazards in prospect rather than consent to a Peace, and peremptorily refuse it, in this case also I wish you were as soon as may be in Portugal, and that you press them to accept the agreement, reasonably accorded in other matters, though but a Truce." Lord Sandwich being then under the mistaken impression that "Spain was likely to grant the title of King in the manner set down in the Projèct mentioned (*i.e.*, in the preface or preamble) so it be for a Truce only, but are obstantly against a Peace."

On $\frac{19}{29}$ April Sir Richard wrote his last despatch to

England dealing at length with his proceedings connected with the treaty of commerce with Spain and the adjustment between that country and Portugal. It was addressed to the Lord Chancellor, and will be found at folio 519, *Harleian MSS.* 7010. In it he reports that the Lord Chancellor's letter of 25 November, 1665, had been delivered to him by Don Patricio Muledi only on $\frac{2}{12}$ April and that he had " no notice of the contents till my arrival in Portugal from Sir Robert Southwell " (on 6-7 February) " being very sorry I had it no sooner; not (as good luck would have it) that I had made any false step in that time in my negotiation with reference to Portugal, having had the happiness to obtain from this Crown on behalf thereof an offer which I carried with me thither (obliging Spain and only Spain, whatever hath been suggested to the contrary from hence, but I hope made no impression in England to my prejudice, being all so contrary to what is evident from the articles themselves which I signed) of all that could seem to me was hoped by the King our Master according to my original instructions, and that in an over-measure and at an under-rate to what is therein expressed and prescribed to me: which conditions I do now perceive even according to your Lo^{ps} said letter, might not only have passed to the content of his majesty, but that his majestys pleasure was that the same (I mean to the same effect) should be pushed on to the utmost in that court before any experiments were made in this to enlarge the Spanish concessions, unless provisionally in case the former would not be accepted.

" But if I had been acquainted with this latter order so soon as I might have been, I would have used all possible endeavours to have gone particularly prepared from hence against the new difficulties I was then to encounter in Portugal in opposition thereunto, anticipating those offices which now in the last resort must be vigorously pursued. . . . All this I presume to say because there are many circumstances inducing me to believe (your Lo^{p} may certainly know it) that

Don Patricio knew the contents of what he brought me from yr. Lo^p^,* so consequently that (admitting it to be so and being himself to come at great leisure) he advertised the same by the swiftest conveyance to the Duke of Medina, with whom I treated. Finally that the Duke might industriously conceal them from me lest the knowledge thereof should divert me from signing together with his Exc^y^ the said articles relating to Portugal upon a mistaken foundation, above intimated, that I by so doing must necessarily oblige my master to cause them to be agreed with on the Portugal side whether liked or not, whereas (for vindication of myself in this point particularly, and concerning my deportment in general with reference to the Portuguese treaty) I have here since my return, after a short preface by word of mouth, put into the Queen's hand a memorial containing quotations of constant undeceptions as to that from time to time throughout the whole course of my treaty. Moreover many days are not passed since I plainly told the Duke (taking notice of that mistaken supposition and reflecting upon that supposed concealment in regard thereof) that if I had received or known the contents of your lordship's letter before I signed the said articles I would have been so far from holding my hand that I should in obedience thereunto much the rather have signed them, as finding thereby it was my Master's express pleasure I should in the first place (go) through trial of that form, and that I should accordingly also have carried them into Portugal and there pressed it to my utmost as I have done; only with this difference that I should have earnestly soliciled to have carried along with me

* The Conde de Molina clearly had the fullest information of what went on in England, and sent his news promptly through Flanders and France, where it was allowed to pass after being duly tapped as being for the most part in the interest of the French aim that they should make the peace between Spain and Portugal on their own terms, or else that no such peace should be made. As will be seen below it must undoubtedly have been treachery on the part of some Spanish authority which prevented the Lord Chancellor's letter of 25 November from reaching Sir Richard Fanshawe.

likewise her Catholick Majestys utmost resolution in case that would not do (as we see it hath happened) concerning the other expedients in your Lordships letter proposal.

"And as your lordships above cited of the 25th of november came so very lately to my hands from Don Patricio, so I must repeat here also (having often noted it before) that a long one in cypher of the 5th of the same from my Lord Arlington (and to the same effect as I conjecture) is not come to this day, having been recommended to an expresse of the Conde de Molina." Sir Richard went on to say that in his apprehension the Spanish ministers would not have any appetite for making an alliance with England until they should see what the success of the summer might be, unless his master should gain suddenly some notable advantage, or the French could no longer disemble with the House of Austria, or Lord Sandwich brought such tempting conditions as would induce them to "swallow at one gulp a pill which is so bitter to them"—a forecast which Lord Sandwich found to be only too true for the space of a whole year when the second alternative came into being. Of course Sir Richard was obliged to add to his letter that he was "reduced to very great exigencies by the failing compliance in my payments out of the Exchequer which is much behindhand with me, notwithstanding that (over and above my Lord Treasurer's universal justice and goodness in these like cases, joined with something of partial indulgence to me) I have at present such subordinate friends in these relations (assisting me hitherto at pinches even beyond a cast of their office) as every public minister abroad must not hope for, or I to hold for ever: such is the diversion caused by the present Wars or the Customary Fate of Ambassadors." Writing on the same point to Lord Arlington on 7 April, N.S. (*Addl. MSS.*, 34, 338, f. 53) Sir Robert Southwell said, "only the Conde Peyneranda and some few justify my Lord Ambassador to the highth, and all the method of his proceedings, and lay the oversight on the Duke, And also judge it hard fortune on the Ambassador that his letter of Novr 5th from your lordship, given to an express of the Conde de Molina, should never be heard of, nor my Lord Chancellor's letter by Don Patricio Muledi of Novr 25th be yet delivered."—And writing on the 10 April to the Earl of Sandwich (f. 35) Sir Robert recorded "The truth is the Spaniards do more highly insist on this point of the King's being obliged by what my Lord Ambassador Fanshawe did, because, if I mistake not in calculation, here was a deep design laid to get the King of England if possible into such a straight; for finding by advice from the Conde de Molina or Don Patriceo Muledi that England would not renounce Portugal, but seemed rather to think it reasonable that Spain should yield the title and a peace, and yet England being the only mediator that Spain could well use in this case, was resolved before England could declare that opinion to them, or that the ambassador here could probably know thereof, to huddle up a treaty with him and that in great secrecy, which was accordingly done, though my Lord Ambassador wanted not care on his side. And that no information from England should interrupt the design, a letter from my Lord Arlington of 5th November delivered to the Conde de Molina to be sent by an express of his, which imported my being designed for Portugal and perhaps somewhat of my errand, was never delivered to the Ambassador. On the 26th November the Lord Chancellor wrote by Don Patricio Muledi a very long letter stating the whole matter and advising him how to proceed; and no doubt but Don Patricio knew the substance of it, as pretending willingness to contribute thereunto, yet advising the court here before he left England what it contained" (tho' he had not yet delivered it since his arrival in Madrid 2 days back) "So that I am verily persuaded they had a plot upon the Ambassador here to invite him to proceed in such a treaty as the King of England should be absolutely bound thereby to make it good or else to renounce Portugal; and it appears by the sequel that although the Ambassador meant nothing less (*i.e.* there was nothing to which the Ambassador meant less to agree), yet the Duke of Medina wholly drove at that point, and declares that he has gained it and that the King in honour is bound to make it good—so that the Ambassador appeals now to his papers and the nature of the negotiations, that a mediator could not bind, and the truth (no doubt) is clear on his side."

It seems almost incredible that Sir Richard Fanshawe should have to complain that no communications were sent to him through the medium of Lord Sandwich and his staff, though it must have been well known in London that several important despatches from there had never reached Madrid. In a letter of $\frac{2}{12}$ May (*Harleian*, 7010, 525), acknowledging one of Lord Arlington's of 5 April, he notes that this was the first he had received since 14 January; and it is quite clear that the failure of the Secretary of State's office to despatch their communications safely to Madrid was quite as great as that of Sir Richard to get his letters home to London.

Six days before the arrival of Lord Sandwich at Madrid, Sir Richard and Sir Robert made another attempt to gain time with Portugal by writing to the Conde de Castel Melhor on 22 May (*Addl. MSS.*, 34, 338, 74) in reply to a communication of his of 3 April, that the delay on their side proceeded altogether from the extraordinary deliberation of the Spanish Court, which had now decided that as the Earl of Sandwich His Majesty's Ambassador Extraordinary was coming to it with ample powers for making a league between that Crown and England, they could not give any positive answer in the matter of adjusting with Portugal until they saw a certainty of the league; and all endeavours to draw an answer sooner "because of the necessity of affairs and the season of the year" had proved unavailing. But they begged the Conde to still incline his master to defer any adjustment with France which might put him out of "a capacity of enjoying that quiet and repose which the King our master so earnestly concerns himself to procure." Will it be believed that the Court of Spain refused a passport for a carrier of this letter, and in consequence it was never sent.

Sir Richard Fanshawe had very cruel bad luck in his Spanish-Portuguese negotiations. He had been reprimanded 5 January, 1664-5 (*Fanshawe Letters*, 430), for intimating on 18 November previous, that he would retire from the Court until he should receive instructions from home, though he had been specially instructed by the Lord Chancellor—as early as 31 July, 1664—to say this if Spain would not allow negotiations for a treaty with England to proceed, and had received the same instructions from the Secretary of State on August 25 which were repeated by the latter on 3 November (*Fanshawe Letters*, 313, 213, 239 and 367). His over-strong action as regards the ambassadorial immunity of his Quarter had been disapproved; and this being most unfortunately reported at the end of October, arrived in England before the proposals for the Anglo-Spanish treaty, which were under discussion between him and the Duke de Medina de las Torres, reached there; and the facts reported were taken advantage of by the Spanish Ambassador at St. James', to challenge his fitness for his post and practically bring about his recall, as detailed above. Then his journey to Portugal was so long deferred by the protracted duration of the negotiations at Madrid that his arrival was contemporaneous with that of the special French Envoy, the Abbé Romain, who made unlimited orders to Portugal not to conclude any agreement with Spain, and by some treachery, for it could not have been less, the Jesuit offers from Badajos spoilt whatever chance there might have been of the proposal of a truce between the Spanish and Portuguese Governments being accepted. Finally when he returned to Madrid with the acceptance to the proposed terms by the Portuguese, provided they were made to them in the form they required, the Spaniards took refuge in the expectation, carefully encouraged by the Spanish minister in England, that Lord Sandwich was bringing terms for them which would save their honour in the matter of acknowledging the title of the King of Portugal. It was clearly impossible in the circumstances that the Duke de Medina de las Torres could consider Sir Richard Fanshawe was the best instrument for arranging terms between Spain and Portugal, now that he no longer had the full support of his own Government, however unfairly withdrawn, and had been told to stay his hand (a fact which of course was known to the Duke through Molina at least),* had been rejected by Portugal, and was now the object of fierce attack at the Spanish Court; and so his failure remained on record until the arrival of Lord Sandwich and the presentation to him of his letters of recall.

The dispute regarding the privilege of the Ambassador's quarter which Lady Fanshawe refers to, December, 1664 (*Memoirs*, p. 161), took place really in the following month, copies of the full correspondence regarding it being among the *Heathcote* MSS., and bearing the dates of 10—13 January, 1665. The hundreds of examples to which she alludes, dwindle down in the correspondence "en favor de mis fueros," to two, one of 1630 in the time of Sir Francis Cottington and one in that of Sir Arthur Hopton. A copy of all the correspondence was sent on the 20th to the Duke de Medina de las Torres, who had intervened in the dispute on being addressed by the Ambassador the day after he made his reference to the President of Castille, the ground for this being that it was feared Don Francisco Ayala would be sent privately into banishment. Sir Richard could only assert that Don Francisco was his neighbour, a wall only dividing them, their two residences having formerly been one.

The Conde de Castrillo simply alleged that no

* On 7 April Sir Richard wrote to Lord Arlington "I do also presume from many circumstances they do already know the full effect beforehand as a thing communicated to the Spanish ministers there upon their own encouragement and in confidence it would here take."

Ambassador had privilege to protect from the ordinary justice outside the doors of his dwelling house.

The question in dispute was by no means so simple a one as Sir Richard asserted; for Wiquefort placed on record in 1740, that the privilege was no part of the law of nations and that Ambassadors could afford safety only with the consent of the Sovereign of the Place, and should be very cautious in doing so unless willing to run the risk of being affronted. He also noted that the considerable immunities once enjoyed by Ambassadors in Spain were abused, and had been reduced.

The reference to the case of the murderers of Anthony Ascham in 1650, in the letter to the Duke, was very general only, the words being "no sea el Rey de Yngl[a] el unico contra quien en espacio de pocos años Espagna ha violada el Sagrado de la Iglesia y el Privilegio de Embaxadores," which throws light on Lady Fanshawe's obscure wording on p. 164 of the *Memoirs*. Another ground the Ambassador gave for troubling the Duke was that "toda la Corte" was "ya llena de mi affrenta."

There were endless disputes about the privilege of Ambassadorial quarters and servants in the XVII century, especially at Madrid. Lord Denbigh threatened to leave Venice over such a difference—the Emperor's Minister at Madrid, Poetting, had great trouble with the Spanish officials regarding his servants—and Marshall Villars demanded privilege for his whole quarter in 1680, which was at first refused but was afterwards yielded. There can be no doubt that the local officials deliberately put affronts on Sir Richard Fanshawe in connection with his servants and that the stiff-necked pride of higher officers of State supported their most outrageous proceedings, and successfully drew the English Representative.

The further complaint which Sir Richard made regarding the inviolability of his quarter arose from circumstances which occurred in the last week of July and were the subject of report to the King of Spain at the end of that month. The person arrested on this occasion was the alguacil attached to the household of the Ambassador, and the President of Castille naturally contended that he did not cease to be subject to the Spanish jurisdiction because of this deputation, the immunity of all Ambassadors at the Court of Spain extending only to their residence and not to their quarter, in which the officers of justice were entitled to proceed with their rods of office. The Council endorsed this view, and it was expressed to the Ambassador by the useful emissary the Baron of Batteville. (*Simancas records.*) Fresh trouble arose soon after the King's death, and was possibly deliberately provoked by the Spanish police. The Council no doubt felt that it was bound to make a firm stand in the matter, if its authority were to be respected, and equally no doubt all the other Ambassadors in Madrid closely watched their action, and that of he English Envoy. Sir Richard finally reported to his Court on $\frac{11}{21}$ October, 1665 (*Harleian*, 7010, f. 412) the long tale of the indignities offered to his servants, and through them to him, by the subordinate agents of Justice in Madrid, and which led ultimately to his depriving an alguazil of his rod of office which he bore through the Ambassadorial quarter. Sir Richard again referred to them in his letter of $\frac{18}{28}$ October, 1665 (*Spanish State Papers*, P.R.O., No. 49). The Council of Regency somehow became aware of the reference made by the Ambassador, and on the $\frac{21}{31}$ October, after drawing attention to the enormity of this action, alleged to have been perpetrated when the minister of justice was in the public street well removed from the Ambassador's residence, and recording that such acts were likely to compromise the negotiations in hand for a treaty between England and Spain, on which the conclusion of an adjustment with Portugal depended, recommended that one of the Secretary's of State should address a strong protest to the Ambassador, and that an express should be at once sent to the Conde de Molina reporting all the facts of the case and instructing him to represent to the King that it was impossible to complete negotiations with a minister who showed such disregard for the wishes of the Court to which he was accredited, and which was determined that the jurisdiction of Ambassadors should not extend beyond the entrance to their residences (*Simancas State Papers*, 2535).*

There had clearly been an earlier despatch than that then sent, for on 13 November the Conde reported from Oxford that in a conversation with Lord Arlington, he had said that he knew the Ambassador had sent ungrounded complaints home and that his actions in Madrid were more likely to provoke war than cement a peace, and in particular his twice threatening to leave the Spanish Court without orders from England.

On the 29 November in continuation of a despatch to Don Blasco de Loyala of the 24th, the Conde reported that the Duke of York had told him the previous evening that though this was not made public, it had been decided to send another Ambassador to Spain, and a fortnight later he wrote (on 12 December), that el General Sandwich had been nominated as Ambassador Extraordinary, adding that no Englishman could have been chosen more likely to conclude peace promptly and plainly. These two letters took the Council by surprise, according to their resolution of 28 January, 1666, which recorded that the letter of 8 November sent to the Conde was merely a precaution against the Ambassador having represented his view of the question of his privilege to his court, and that it gave him no lead to suggest or ask for his recall, and accordingly recommended that the Duke de Medina de Las Torres should write to Sir Richard Fanshawe and state that the Queen had full confidence in him,† and that the Conde de Molina

* The Resolutions of the Council referred also to the excesses committed by the household of the Ambassador of France and the Resident of Modena.

† This apparently had some foundation in fact, for in Sir Richard's official letter home, dated 4 November s.n. (Oct. 25 O.S.), he had reported that on the occasion of his interview with

should be ordered to proceed to Flanders and explain his conduct from there as nothing less would suffice to reassure him.*

Lady Fanshawe's letter of $\frac{18}{28}$ January to her husband (*Heathcote* MSS. 225) shows that the Duke of Medina de las Torres informed her very fully what had taken place in Council over the news of the coming of the Earl of Sandwich and the censure of the Conde de Molina, and that she completely grasped the whole situation in spite of her demure answer to the Duke that she was "not capacitated to understand the things of state." Lady Fanshawe's words of comfort to her husband in this great trouble which was befalling him, and of which she was well able to judge, are very brave and sweet. "Be cheerful my soul and as thou hast always had God and honour before thy eyes, so thou wilt never want his blessing thereupon"—"Be cheerful, make much of thy self . . . be not too thoughtful, but do the best that in thee lies for God's glory, for thy country's good and thy own honour and profit, and then submit cheerfully to God's decrees"—and again "if thou mayst be so happy to conclude the business now, or to lay there a foundation so as to do it hereafter in this place, it will be most happy; if not God's will be done to whom I perpetually pray that he will bless, preserve and keep thee, and send us a happy meeting. Thyn ever Ann Fanshawe" (*Letter* of $\frac{2}{12}$ Feb.).

The Council was of course divided in its opinion: the Duke de Medina de las Torres, the Marquis of Velada, the Conde of Ayala and the Dukes of Alberquerque, and Montalto, were of opinion that the Spanish Ambassador should be ordered to Flanders to explain his conduct. The Conde de Penaranda, the Duke of Alba, Cardinal Colonna, and the Confessor of

the Queen on that day, she had told him "that she had given strict orders for all Ministers of Justice to carry themselves towards me and mine hereafter with that respect which is due to my representation" (*Harleian* MSS., 7010, f. 427).

* Molina was in London on 24 April, 1665; he had left Ostend on Monday 13th, Dover 14th, London 16th, saw the King and and Queen on the 18th, and the Queen mother on the 19th.

the Queen, Nethard, while agreeing that the Conde de Molina had, without authority "por capricho suyo" thought that he should not be recalled until the facts of the case were more fully known, suggesting that Lord Sandwich was being sent only on a special embassy of condolence on the King's death and that Fanshawe was not being recalled—all were agreed that a letter should be at once sent to Fanshawe assuring him of the Queen's esteem and trust. The weaker line was of course adopted, Fanshawe being informed as above, an assurance destroyed by the explanation that Molina's unauthorised action had been taken by reason of the differences which had arisen in Madrid in connection with Ambassadorial differences there, and that it was due to the dignity of Ambassadors that Molina should not be recalled until he had reported more fully upon the action taken by him, and that Sandwich was probably coming on an embassy of condolence (*Simanca's Records*). These papers show that though the Duke of Medina may have been speaking of what he had recommended in his conversation with Lady Fanshawe, reported in her letter of 28 January (*Heathcote MSS.*, p. 225), his Secretary certainly told her untruthfully on 3 February (p. 229), that Conde "Moliney" was recalled and would be in Madrid in a few days to answer for his insolent action. It appears from a letter of the Margues of Castel Rodrigo of the date of 11 March, from Brussels, that he intervened on behalf of Molina, who had been Quarter-Master General in Flanders, and bade him keep any orders of censure or recall secret, till further orders came, and urged the Queen to take no further steps against the appointment of Sandwich; and no doubt the advice of the men whom Spain trusted to somehow see them through the impending troubles with France, carried great weight with the council, which decided to let the whole matter drop in spite of the promises to Sir Richard Fanshawe.

Well might the Preface to the Letters (published in 1724) "on divers matters of importance between the three crowns of England Spain and Portugal" 1663-1678, record: "I need give no character of the Spanish Court here; the negotiations then carried on with them will do it effectually in this book, and it is satyr sufficient upon that subject; A stiff haughty wary people, weak in council as in arms; taken up with punctilios and ceremony, jealous and tedious in negotiating, and dilitory in executing what they resolve upon; this character of the Spaniards runs through every part of this work."

Lord Sandwich records in his Journal that one of his footmen was killed in rudely pursuing four alguaçils upon a rumour that they had passed "through our barriers with their rods exalted, which by custom they ought not to do," and that another alguacil who served a process in a house within the barriers was only reprimanded, and not cashiered and sent to beg mercy as "I justly expected."

Sandwich also records that, on the occasion of the public reception of another Venetian Ambassador, the French laqueys came with arms under their coats to dispute his precedence, if he should send his coach for the function.

The offensive and defensive league between Portugal and France was signed on 21 March, 1667, and the commercial treaty between England and Spain on 1 May, copies of the latter being interchanged on 13 May (*Sandwich Journals*). The first copies sent home miscarried; the third, by the hands of Henry Sheres, arrived in September and was read in Council on the 9th. Sheres left again with the ratified treaty on 15 October, and reached Madrid early in November, where its conclusion was duly celebrated on the 30th of that month; meanwhile the peace of Breda had been signed on 21 July, and the Spanish feigned assurance of safety from French hostilities came to an abrupt end. The Queen at once informed Sandwich that Spain would yield the title of King to Portugal. The Earl thereupon proposed to proceed on the basis of Sir Richard Fanshawe's project of February, 1666, informing the Conde de Peñaranda that he had by him "a treaty made at Salvatierra by my Lord Fanshaw whereunto the Conde Castel Melhor had by order set his hand; and for the acceptance of which by the King of Portugal we had security from him last winter, so that we had reason to think the matter of that project would please now." Then in the very nick of time came, first the banishment of the Conde de Castel Melhor, the only able minister round the King; and next the deposition of the King himself; and the murder of the Marquess of Sande, the one prominent upholder of the French Alliance, added further advantage for the Spanish negotiations; and in the end, what had proved impossible in the early months of 1666, matured into actuality in those months of 1668; the Spanish Portuguese treaty being signed on 3 February just three weeks after Lord Sandwich reached Lisbon, and the ratifications of it were exchanged on the 23rd *idem*. Barely two months later, by the peace of Aachen, Spain yielded to France all the demands made of her. Further than this, it is not necessary here to follow the negotiations in connection with the commercial treaty between Spain and England and the peace between the former and Portugal. They are fully treated in the Appendix to the Edition of the *Memoirs* of 1907, and nothing which has come to light since, either from Home or Foreign State Records or from Lord Sandwich's Journals, necessitates any modification of the views expressed there.* Until France declared War on Spain, who was thus brought face to face with ruin, and until the revolution in Portugal mitigated the stiff neckedness of that country, Lord Sandwich was no more able to make any effectual progress towards the accomplishment of the mission on which he was sent, than Sir Richard

* A number of attempts to ascertain if any public records of the time which may still remain in Lisbon contain any mention of the Embassies of Sir Richard Fanshawe to Portugal, have all resulted in complete failure.

Fanshawe had been able to do during the two years previous to June, 1666, in spite of the fact that the support he received from England was of a very different quality from that accorded to his predecessor. Lord Sandwich himself, when the Queen announced that she would yield in the matter of the title of King after the "ill accident of the King of France, his falling upon Flanders and Catalonia," did Sir Richard the justice to record in his diary in September, 1667, "It is good to peruse a memorial of my Lord Fanshaw to the Queen (upon his return from Portugal with that projèct and letter of Conde Castel Melhor) wherein he shows the likelihood for giving satisfaction in these particulars, and that they could not prejudice the adjustment."

The rest of the stay of Sir Richard and Lady Fanshawe in Madrid, until his death on 26 June and her departure on 8 July, is dealt with by her in the *Memoirs* only very briefly, the chief events recorded relating to her farewell visits to the Court, the marriage and departure of the Empress, and the arrival of the Ambassador Extraordinary, the Earl of Sandwich. The diary of the latter contains, however, a number of interesting details of the time, which are here given by the kind permission of the late Earl. Lord Sandwich sailed from Spithead on 2 March, 1666, and reached Corunna on 12 March (O.S.), 14 days after Sir Richard had returned to Madrid; news of his arrival was sent off the same day by the Governor Don Pedro Martinez and was received at Madrid on the $\frac{16\text{th}}{26\text{th}}$. On the $\frac{20\text{th}}{30\text{th}}$ both Sir Richard, and Sir Robert Southwell wrote welcoming him, and their letters were received by him on 5 April; meanwhile on the $\frac{20}{30}$ March the Earl had despatched Mr. Werden from Corunna: Sir Richard had an interview with him from a distance on $\frac{28\text{ March}}{7\text{ April}}$ at Chamartin (*Memoirs*, p. 552), and he took back a letter of the $\frac{1}{11}$ April (*Harleian* 7010, f. 495). This reached Lord Sandwich on the $\frac{7\text{th}}{17\text{th}}$, who finding the preparations made by the Court for his journey to be very insufficient, despatched his personal Secretary Dr.

Taylor to Madrid on the 11th. The Memoirs do not mention this incident, but Sir Richard refers to the visit in his letter of $\frac{22\text{ April}}{2\text{ May}}$ (*Memoirs*, p. 552) in which he begged the Earl to let him know if he brought letters of revocation for him. Lord Sandwich notes that his letter reached him on $\frac{29\text{ April}}{9\text{ May}}$, and that on the $\frac{5}{15}$ May he had replied, " upon his earnestly pressing me to a catagorical answer " that he " acknowledged the having of such letters for him, but would advise still to be kept secret until we had seen one the other." Meanwhile the marriage of the Empress on Easter Sunday $\frac{15}{25}$ April had happened; the private audience granted an hour before it to Sir Richard (*Memoirs*, p. 556) is not mentioned by Lady Fanshawe, though the public audience accorded to him and Sir Robert Southwell two days later is duly recorded by her: the whole account of this and of the marriage and of the departure of the Empress is taken bodily from the report of Sir Richard dated $\frac{18}{28}$ April (*Harleian* MSS. 7010).

Lady Fanshawe had taken leave of the Queen of Spain and Empress and the King on the $\frac{1}{11}$ April and the next day of the *camarera mayor*, and of the King's *aya* (*Memoirs*, p. 187). The original letters of the Ladies of the bedchamber of the Queen and Empress, dated Thursday and Friday, 8 and 9 April, for the visits of Lady Fanshawe and her daughters to their mistress and themselves on Sunday, and to themselves on Monday, were among the *Heathcote MSS.* The explanation of this special reception becomes clear from the *Memoires Curieux* of Carel, one of the entourage of the Archbishop of Embrun, which, however, contain hardly anything of interest. In them it is stated with doubtful truth that the English Ambassador sought to be present at the marriage of the Infanta. The Council advised that only those who had the right of entry to the Royal Chapel should be invited, but the Queen decided that no Ambassadors should be present, thus favouring the English Representative. It seems much more probable that the Nuntio, and other Ambassadors representing Roman Catholic Princes, were present at the marriage on Easter day.

On May $\frac{7}{17}$ Lord Sandwich left the Quinta of Burgos, just outside Corunna, in which he had spent his quarantine from 15 March, and on Friday $\frac{18th}{28th}$, as he records, " went from hence (Torre Lodones) 10 miles to El Pardo a house of the King's where my Lord Ambassador ffanshaw, Sir Robert Southwell English Envoy, and Don Alonso Antonio de Paz, Master of the Ceremonies with three of the Queen's coaches, and Mr. Godolphin " [?Goddard] " and many other merchants and English came to meet me; and after a little repast we went straight to Madrid thence 6^{m}, to the house prepared for me, a very noble one," where the Duke of Medina de las Torres at once presented his compliments through Don Patricio Muledi.

The following are the Diary entries of the next two days the $\frac{19}{29}$ and $\frac{20}{30}$ May :—

Saturday 19th: " My Lord Ambassador ffanshaw came to me in the morning when I gave him my Lord Arlington's private letter. I discussed with him according to my instructions, desiring of him an account of the state of His majesty's affairs, and letting him know the condition of the treaty of commerce being not ratified, and upon what grounds; and in the afternoon Sir Richard ffanshaw and Mr. Godolphin and I took the papers and particularly ran through the exceptions and heard his Lordship's reply to them. He pressed me in the close to tell him what letters I had for his revocation, which I did."

" Sunday 20th (May): In the afternoon my Lord Ambassador ffanshaw and I again discussed our points of commerce, and in the close he desired me to deliver his letters of revocation, the which I did." Lady Fanshawe mentions the delivery as on the date of the 19th. A marginal note to the diary entry of that date states that Sir Richard's replies were to be found in the 2nd Volume of the Journal and they are those printed on pages 244-5 of the *Memoirs*. On 22 May it was resolved Sir Richard should apply for a private reception of the Embassador Extraordinary by the Queen before his public one; the application was made by Sir Richard the same day (*Heathcote* MSS., p. 253) and was granted on Sunday 27th, at half-past seven in the evening, Sir Richard Fanshawe introducing him. Lord Sandwich recording the fact under that date and that the "Queen made some return in a few words respectful to my master and favourable to me, and said she would appoint with whom I was to treat."* Lady Fanshawe is wrong in her chronology here, as she states that her husband's banquet in honour of the King's birthday was given before this interview, whereas, of course, it took place on 29 May, two days later, as Lord Sandwich duly notes, terming the entertainment "a noble treat and collation at 6 o'clock in the evening," the Master of Ceremonies and Don Patricio Muledi being present and many of the English merchants, as well as the Ambassador Extraordinary and all his comerades. To this slip Lady Fanshawe adds another, viz., that the private interview was granted on Whit Sunday (instead of the Sunday before). Whit Sunday fell on $\frac{3}{13}$ June, it was on this day that Sir Richard received the Communion for the last time before his illness.

On Whit Monday he accompanied Lord Sandwich on a formal visit to the Duke of Medina de las Torres, and on the next day ($\frac{5\text{th}}{15\text{th}}$) he fell sick of the fever, which killed him, as noted in the *Memoirs*. Lord Sandwich records on 6 June, Wednesday, "my Lord Fanshawe fell sick being struck with a cold air, as he slept after dinner: one was killed outright in the

* Lord Sandwich's request for a private audience before his public one caused a great flutter in the ambassadorial dovecots in Madrid, and the Venetian minister favoured his Signoria with two long letters on the subject, which as usual, where mischief making was concerned, was hotly taken up by the Archbishop of Embrun. In his report on the meeting of the British Ambassador with the Ambassador Extraordinary, Marin Zorzi had recorded that they interchanged but few words and that the countenance of the former was full of sorrow—no doubt imaginary details, provided by the fancy of the spectator of the rencontre at El Pardo.

Henry Bennet, Earl of Arlington

Engraving from a portrait by Sir Peter Lely

LBBD Archives at Valence House

Edward Montagu, Earl of Sandwich

Engraving from a portrait by Sir Peter Lely

LBBD Archives at Valence House

same manner that day." A detailed account of Sir Richard's sickness and death* is given from the records among the *English State Papers* at pages 562-3 of the *Memoirs*, the most pathetic notice being that of his Chaplain Mr. Bagshaw in the Funeral Sermon of 4 July quoted on p. 567 of the *Memoirs*. The following details are added from other domestic sources and the despatches of the ministers of other Courts residing at Madrid. Lord Sandwich wrote in his Journal " Hearing that the Physicians despaired of my Lord Fanshaw's life I went to see him after dinner and found him in a dying condition. As soon as he saw me he lifted his hands upward 2 or 3 times (having not spoken for an hour before) to signify he was going to heaven, and then striving to speak said This was the end of this world. and said I submit, I submit. The Duke and Duchess of Aveiro were to see him in the morning and she brought with her relicks which she believed to have done great miracles, and laid them upon the pillow by him out of good will; but this together with a Friar's (Father Duffy's) presence gave occasion for a report in Madrid that he had been confessed and received the Sacrament in the Romish way. In the afternoon came the Dukes of Aveiro and Monterey sent from the Queen to visit him and the Master of the Ceremonies and brought a priest with them. When they came into the room Mr. Bagshaw my Lord Ambassador's Chaplain was kneeling by his bed side, but the Priest pressed towards the bed and over his shoulder told him that if he would confess he was come to give him absolution; but my Lord flung away his hands and expressed much dislike. My Lady Fanshawe being in another room and hearing discourse about such a matter stept in and complained that they should trouble my lord at such

* Sir Richard Fanshawe died in the same month as that in which he was born 58 years before. Lady Fanshawe must have thought of it :—

" Nature is out of tune
The world is sick and like to die in June."

Pastor Fido, Act I., Scene 1.

a time who had composed himself to die in the faith he had professed when he was in perfect health and judgement and desired they would desist. Whereupon the Dukes went away, but then came the master of the Ceremonies and would have introduced the priest again, but they would not suffer it. Mr. Bagshaw my Lord's Chaplain had before this visit asked my Lord (for) a declaration of what faith he died in, and he replied, the faith of the Church of England; but after this attempt* he again desired him to declare it before many of his family, and he again said, he died in the faith of the Church of England. And about 11 oclock this night my Lord Ambassador Fanshaw died."

The account given by Lord Sandwich is fully corroborated by Mr. Parry in a letter of 1 July, 1666, to Sir Robert Southwell (*Addl. MSS.* 34, 338, f. 38), in which he says that Sir Richard Fanshawe took leave of his wife and children about noon, and died at eleven of the night "enjoying both his reason and senses to the last. My Lady asked of him whether he would be buried in Hertfordshire or at Westminster, and he replied at Westminster." Mr. Godolphin in a letter to the same and of the same date (f. 37) also mentions the desire to be interred in Westminster Abbey.†

On 30 June the Venetian Ambassador, Sir Richard's old opponent, reporting to their Serenities, recorded that though Don Ricardo Fanshau Ambassador Ordinary of England was of some age, yet he was strong and vigorous; he had, however, been depressed in spirit by the trouble which had befallen him, and which had

* These attempts may be compared with those at the death bed of the Earl of Roscommon (*Memoirs,* p. 402). It was on account of them no doubt that Lady Fanshawe specially recorded of her husband (*Memoirs,* p. 4): "He was a true Protestant of ye Church of England, so borne, so brought up, and so dyed." "Qualis vita, finis ita. La tarde loa el dia, y el fin la vida."

† Of men who were much on an equality with Sir Richard, his cousin Lord Hatton, Sir Robert Long, Sir Allan Apsley, Sir Robert Howard and Sir William Temple, were buried in Westminster Abbey, and among his more distinguished contemporaries, Lord Cottington, the Earls of Sandwich and Clarendon and the Duke of Ormonde.

struck him to the heart. He notes that the attempt of the Religiosi was repelled by the wife and Chaplain (Predicante) of the dying man, who thus passed away in the bonds of false belief and perdition. Count Fuente records in his diary that Sir Richard "fallecio (died) Puritano Fortificato en esto mucho su mujer no apartandose jamas de su lado." In his despatch of 2 July (*Fontes Rerum Austriacarum* LVI., 235) he wrote "Der ordentliche englische Gesandte ist vor einigen tagen gestorben, und zwar in seinem puritanischen Glauben"; to which the Emperor Leopold I. responded "Quod pauper ille Anglus in sua non angelica sed impura Puritana hœresi obiit. condoleo ejus animae."

The funeral service held for Sir Richard upon 4 July was on a Sunday. Mr. Parry records that Lady Fanshawe was greatly angered by the Queen's offer to provide for her if she and her children would become Roman Catholics, and Lord Sandwich states on the $\frac{\text{28 June}}{\text{8 July}}$ that, "This evening my Lady Fanshawe went away with her family from Madrid"; seventeen days later he moved into her house of the Siete Chimineas, and on 27 July mentions the receipt of the pass granted to her by the Duke of Beaufort from Lisbon, on $\frac{12}{22}$ July.

There is nothing special to note regarding her journey from Madrid, by sea from Bilboa to Bayonne, and thence by land to Calais, and so by sea to London where she landed on Tuesday, 12 November, except that among the *Heathcote MSS.* was a passport granted to her by Cornelis de Montigny de Clarges, Agent of the States General at Calais, reciting that Her Excellency held a a pass from the King of France, to pass unmolested by land and sea with her children and 30 domestics and the coffined body of her husband, Ambassador of the King of England to the King of Spain, where he died, and directing all Captains and other officers of their Highnesses to let her pass to London. The direct route from Tower Hill to Lincoln's Inn Fields lay through the area utterly destroyed by the Fire of London; but Lady

Fanshawe probably proceeded round the line of London Wall or else by the Tower to the Temple Stairs. (It is somewhat curious that she never mentions the Thames in her Memoirs except on the occasion of her flight to Gravesend and France in 1659.)

As noted on p. 575 of the *Memoirs* the body of her husband was buried temporarily in All Saints, Hertford on 27 November, 1666. In the 5th year after, on the anniversary of their wedding day, it was transferred to the vault which Lady Fanshawe had caused to be made in St. Mary's Chapel on the south side of the parish church at Ware. It having become necessary to restore the floor of that chapel it was decided to fill up the vault, and the writer of this history was present when the vault was reverently opened on 9 March, 1908 and again closed. It was found to contain the leaden coffin of Sir Richard with a plate of glass at the head of the upper surface, through which the bones inside could be seen, and the hasps and locks were there which had once protected the outer coffin, made so that the lid of it could be raised according to the custom of Spain as noted in the case of King Philip IV. at page 179-80 of the *Memoirs*; the vault also contained another leaden coffin, apparently that of a man, without any indication as to who the person buried in it was, and a number of bones from some coffins which had completely decayed away: among these was a skull of a woman, which may have been that of Lady Fanshawe. It was found that the vault had been opened before and unduly disturbed, a portion of it being portioned off in 1820 as the last resting place of Sophia Langden, wife, or possibly daughter, of the Vicar of the Church from 1791 to 1832. The vault was of unusual size being 14 feet long by 8½ feet broad and 7 feet high to the corner of the arch. An account of the opening of it was published by one of the church-wardens of the church, Mr. R. B. Croft, of Farhams Hall, Ware.*

* It it a curious coincidence that the bodies of both the Ambassador Ordinary and the Ambassador Extraordinary of England, who were together in Madrid in May and June, 1666,

Ann Lady Fanshawe (1625-80), in widowhood

by Mary Beale

Valence House Museum

St Mary's Church, Ware

LBBD Archives, Valence House

Nothing special has come to light regarding the life of Lady Fanshawe after her return to England. The *Heathcote MSS.* record that she gave up her lease of the Queen Mother's manors of Hitchin and Tring in February, 1669, and the lease of her house at Hertingfordbury in 1672, and took up her residence in East Barnet. In her will she speaks of Faunton Hall in North Bemfleet (Benfleet), Essex. The lease to her husband was dated July, 1661, and that of Fauntonbury —the same place—for 21 years to herself in June, 1668. This lease was held of the Bishop of London and was renewed to her daughter Katherine.

Lady Fanshawe's pitiful petition of 1666, submitting her claim for payment of moneys due to her husband, is printed at p. 576 of the *Memoirs*. In a subsequent petition of 1668, praying that the 8000 oz. of silver plate issued to the Ambassador to Spain from the Jewel House might be allowed to her, she states that she was granted only £5900 out of the amount claimed, and had to pay £400 fees for this sum, and that she sold her tallies for it to Alderman Backwell for £5000, and thus received only £4600 out of £6900 actually spent or due. She urged moreover that her husband had suffered a loss of £1500 by the fall of brass money in Spain (*Memoirs*, p. 153) and the high price of food in Madrid, which she had omitted by an oversight in her original claim. In November, 1668, she submitted a special petition praying for the grant of the additional £1000 which she claimed as the half cost of her journey home from Madrid with her family, and which Lord Arlington had promised "should be considered one way or other" (*Memoirs*, p. 577). In January, 1669 (*Calendar of Treasury Books*, 1669-72) she appeared before the Lord Commissioners in connection with the plate of the

should have been brought home to their last resting place by sea, and by the great highway of the Thames—Sir Richard Fanshawe to the Tower Wharf on 13 November, 1666; and the Earl of Sandwich, after his heroic death in the battle of Southwold Bay, to Westminster Stairs and Hall, and so to the Great Abbey on 3 July, 1672.

Treasury, and they naturally informed her that it must be returned to the Jewel House unless the King should be pleased to order to the contrary. It appeared then that the plate had been broken up for transport by land, as transport by sea was not considered safe; and in April Lady Fanshawe was called upon to Pay £2000 in lieu of returning it. After a struggle to retain half of this money as still due to her on account of the expense of her return home, she paid £1000 and then £500 at the end of April and the beginning of May, and apparently she was required to pay the remaining £500 also, and received her final discharge in July.*

In January of the following year she was again a petitioner " that your majesty will be graciously pleased to give her son Sir Richard Fanshawe, who is altogether unprovided for, the next reversion (after those your Majesty hath already granted) of a teller's place in your Majesty's Exchequer, that so hee being provided for your Majesty's petitioner may be enabled to procure some small portions for her daughters, three whereof are grown up to woman's estate."† Four years later, in September, 1674, a royal warrant directed a grant under the Great Seal of a Surveyorship of Small Customs to Sir Richard

* In October, 1667, five months after successfully concluding his Treaty of Commerce, Lord Sandwich was forced to represent that he owned £5000 and could not get a penny in Madrid without pawning the King's Plate and was indeed " at the last Gasp of Subsistence." (*Fanshawe Letters,* 1724, II., 83). Sir William Godolphin was reduced to even greater straits and protested in April, 1672 (*do.* p. 168) that he was due nearly £3000 of arrears of salary, and did not know how to eat without pawning the very furniture of his house.

† Among the most wonderful efforts of spelling, in her letters of early 1666 to her husband, which appear in Lady Fanshawe's modernised correspondence published at pp. 224-240 of the *Heathcote MSS.*, the following may be quoted—caues for cause, incouredgment for encouragement, likuis and liquies for likewise, thowes for those, sarvice for service, ocation for occasion, lage for league, a monkest for amongst, lam for lamb, sifer for cypher, gras for grace, privet for private, onerabell for honourable, falt for fault, suer for sure, pease for peace, macke for make, hapeyns for happens, lafed for laughed, mach for match, pepell for people, amvoyé for envoyé, dobell for double, frutt for fruit, kipe for keep. It will be seen that not a few of these quaint forms are due to the difference of pronunciation in the XVII. century. Castle Decampaye for Casa del Campo is rather a notable achievement in phonetic spelling.

Fanshawe, then aged 19; and the patent of this appointment, dated 4 December, 1674, is noticed at p. 532 of the *Memoirs.* It is a document of immense length, which is not quite correctly summarised there, the grant being made to Rich. Mountney, jun., Wm Waterson, and Philip Marsh, in reversion after George Porter (son or grandson of Endymion Porter) and Sir John Stapeley,* to hold in trust and solely for the benefit of Sir Richard Fanshawe. As noted there, the post never fell in during the life time of the grantee, as Sir John Stapeley lived till 1701, and he never therefore derived any benefit from it. As with Charles II. of Spain it was "woe to thee, O land, when thy King is a child" (*Ecclesiastes* X. 16)—so with Sir Richard Fanshawe the second Baronet, it was, "Guay (alas) al hijo, cujo padre va a parayso."

Lady Fanshawe desired in her will that she should be buried in the vault in St. Mary's Chapel in Ware Church, close to her husband's body. The parish register records her burial on 20 January, 1679-80. No memorial was raised to her at the time, but in 1905 one was put up to her memory in St. Mary's chapel by members of the Fanshawe Family. This tablet is reproduced in the *Memoirs*.

Ann Fanshawe

Signature of Lady Fanshawe, *from the original MS. of her Memoirs.*

Sir Richard and Lady Fanshawe had six sons and eight daughters; of these, five sons and four daughters died as children. They were, Harrison, born in February, 1644-5 and died 15 days later; Ann, the little daughter

* G. E. Cokayne notes in the Complete Baronetage that Sir John's wealth was derived largely from his post in the Customs.

"Nan" of whom the father and mother were so fond, born in June 1646 and died while they were at Tankersley Park, in July, 1654, aged 8; Henry, born in 1647 and died about two years later; Richard, the little boy whose charming portrait taken with his father,* is still at Dengie Hall, born on 8 June, 1648, and died in Paris in October, 1659, at the age of 11, of whom Lady Fanshawe pathetically says in her Memoirs, "though I neglected ym" (her two little girls aged 6 and 7, who were suffering from the same illness) "& day & night tended my dear son, yet it pleased God they recovered and he dyed"; Elizabeth, born at Madrid on 13 June, 1650 and died on 26th of the same month, followed by another Elizabeth born on 24 June, 1651, who lived to the age of 5 and died in July, 1656; the three children who succeeded these—all daughters—survived their parents; the next child was Mary, the attractive baby whose portrait with her mother was painted by Teniers. She was born on 12 July, 1656, and lived only four years, dying in August, 1660; a year younger was a son in whom the name Henry was revived, he was born in November and died on 2 December, 1657; and on 26 June, 1663, was born a son who again received the father's name, Richard, but only lived a few hours.

The only children who survived Lady Fanshawe besides the three girls already mentioned), were another daughter Elizabeth, born in 1662, and her youngest child, the "most dear and only son" to whom she dedicated her Memoirs.

Very little has been gathered respecting the lives of Sir Richard's daughters.

* It is remarkable how much pictorial illustration exists of the times of Sir Richard and Lady Fanshawe. In portraiture we have the works of Vandyk, Janssens, Lely, Wright and other British artists, and of Velasquez, and a number of French, Flemish and Dutch engravings; for ships and shipping we have Vandervelde and Dirk Stoop; for places and countries we have the quaint series of Delices de Grande Bretagne, France, d'Espagne, Les Pays Bays; the travels of Cosmo de Medici Grand Duke of Tuscany, in England; and many old prints of London and the other principal cities of Great Britain, which give us a clear idea of how they and the buildings in them, appeared to the eyes of those who viewed them in the XVII. century.

Richard Fanshawe (1648-59), third son of Sir Richard Fanshawe

Unknown artist, British (English) School

Valence House Museum

Ann Fanshawe (b.1654), daughter of Sir Richard Fanshawe

Style of Sir Peter Lely

Valence House Museum

Katherine, who was born in Chancery Lane on 30 July, 1652, sold the property at East Barnett as her mother's executrix, on 28 May, 1680, for £1800. The lease of (the manor of) ffanton als ffaunton Berry, held of the Bishop of London, was dated 12 May, 1685, and appears to have included lands called Brownes Lands als Campis Lands situated in North Benfleet, Wickford, Rawreth and elsewhere in Essex; this she surrendered to the Bishop about the year 1690.

As a child she and her sisters accompanied their parents to the Courts of Portugal and Spain; among the *Heathcote* MSS. are two letters in Spanish written by her and her sister Margaret in 1666 to their father, and it appears that the little girls had been learning their father's translation of the *Querer por solo querer*, which, in a letter to their mother, he expresses a desire to hear them repeat. Katherine is the little lady to whom John Bulteel alludes when writing to her father on 22 December, 1665, when he speaks of Sir Richard's "faire Daughters especially Shee that when I had ye honour to dinne with her at your L^ps in Lincolnes Inn fields defied all man-kind and thought of nothing but a Nunnery from which resolution, if her yeares and value of the World hath not by this time redeemed hir yours and my Ladyes authority must or you will have a Sinne to answer for the brave youth of England will never pardon you." Probably Mr. Bulteel is referring to the year 1660 when Sir Richard was living in Lincoln's Inn Fields at which time his little daughter was 8 years old.

After her mother died, Katherine Fanshawe lived first with the Duchess of Albemarle, and later (1681) with Lady Denby (*Rutland* MSS.). She was living unmarried in 1719, but the date of her death is unknown.

Margaret,* the only daughter of Lady Fanshawe who was married in her mother's lifetime, became the wife of Vincent Grantham of Goltho by Wragby, Lincolnshire,

* Donna Maria de Guzman, Lady Abbess of Alcantra, writing to welcome Sir Richard on $\frac{2}{12}$ February, 1664, speaks of the baby, to whom she is sending a present, as "my precious Margaret." (*Heathcote* MSS.).

on 13 June, 1675, the ceremony taking place in East Barnet church. She was then 21⅔ years of age, having been born in October, 1653, at Tankersley Park. One of the trustees of her marriage settlement was Sir Thomas Fanshawe of Jenkins. She and her husband had a large family of twelve children or more, of whom Vincent, baptized August, 1676 (d. 1688), Richard, baptized 8 October, 1677, and Thomas, baptized November, 1678, were born before their maternal grandmother died.

Margaret Grantham was buried at Goltho on 16 November, 1705, and her husband (who was J.P. for Lindsay in 1678) was buried there on 21 December, 1721. Two sons only survived them, Richard, who died in January, 1722, and a younger Vincent born in 1692, who died in 1758, and was recorded as "the Last male Heir of the family," on his tombstone which still exists in Laceby church.*

The next daughter, born at Frogpool, Kent, on 22 February, 1654-5, was "named Ann to keep in remembrance her dear sister, which we had newly lost" (*Memoirs*, p. 84). An old memorandum at Parsloes states that she married Mr. Ryder, and her uncle Sir Edmond Turnor mentions her as "Ann Ryder Fanshawe alias Ryder" in his will (1704), but the date of her marriage has not been ascertained. It must, however, have taken place between 28 May, 1680—when her signature appears on a release to her sister Katherine—and 1685, when her daughter Ann Ryder was born: the

* The Grantham family was of great antiquity, their arms, Ermine, a griffin segreant gules armed and langued azure, having been granted in 1139. Sir John Grantham was Lord Mayor of London in 1328, and in the two centuries following three of his descendants were Mayors of Lincoln. The last of these, Mayor in 1557, was also Member of Parliament. He married Mary, daughter of Sir John Dunham, of Kirklington, Notts, and his son Vincent married Elizabeth, daughter of Sir Francis Ascough, of Stallington. The son of the latter, Sir Thomas Grantham, made Knight in 1603, married Frances, daughter of Sir John Puckering, Lord Keeper; and their son Thomas, who succeeded in 1630, married Dorothea, daughter of Sir William Alford, of Meux, Yorkshire. Sir Thomas was Sheriff of the county in 1600, and his son in 1639. Four years later the latter was indited for high treason, by the Parliament party no doubt, and died about 1655. His daughter Dorothy, sister of Vincent Grantham, married Henry Hildyard, of Kelstone, Yorkshire, in 1664, and died in 1667.

latter being said to be of the age of 14 at the time when her marriage licence with "John Lawrence of Westminster, gent.," was granted in 1699. "Ann Lawrence, daughter of niece Ryder" was left a legacy under the will of Sir Edmond Turnor. It is supposed that Lady Fanshawe's great grand-daughter, Charlotte Coleman, whose will is dated 6 September, 1766, and was proved in 1768, was the daughter of Ann Lawrence. The edition of *Lady Fanshawe's Memoirs* published in 1829 was taken from a copy of the transcript made by Charlotte Coleman in 1766.

A good deal of mystery surrounds Ann Ryder; many efforts have been made to trace the later part of her life but without much success. Mr. Ryder seems to have disappeared in 1691, as in the daughter's above mentioned marriage licence, it is stated that nothing had been heard of him for 8 years.

Nothing is known of the remaining daughter, Elizabeth, born in Portugal Row, London, on 22 February, 1661-2, beyond her marriage to Christopher Blount. The marriage licence, dated 20 April, 1684, and giving St. Sepulchre's as the church where the marriage was to be celebrated, describes the bridegroom as of the Middle Temple and gives his age as 30. There is no Christopher Blount on the books of the Middle Temple in 1684, nor was his name among those of the law students at King's Inns, Dublin, nor T.C.D., nor on the Irish Law lists. It was not an uncommon thing for non-members to live within the Temple, however, and if he did live there how else could he describe himself in the licence? An old memorandum at Parsloes stated that the wife died in 1720 but there is no confirmation of this.

Sir Richard Fanshawe, second Baronet, at whose death the Baronetcy became extinct, was the youngest child of Lady Fanshawe; he was born at Madrid on 6 August, 1665, six weeks after the Spanish defeat at Montes Claros and as many before the death of the Spanish King; Lady Fanshawe was then in her 41st year and her husband in his 58th. Loving references to him are made by his mother in her letters to her husband, preserved among the *Heathcote MSS.*, in one of which she writes (Feb. 12 1666) "Dick . . . grows a lovely fine boy." He was naturalised as an infant by the desire and direction of his father though the children of an Ambassador (employed by the King in foreign countries) are no aliens. Nothing fresh regarding the second Baronet has come to light since 1907. In a deed dated 10 July, 1688, he is described as of Westminster.

He was buried at St. James's, Clerkenwell, the entry in the church Register being under 12 July, 1694, "Sr Richard Fanshawe, K^t^ was buried the same day South Ile from Wood's Close." In Pink's *History of Clerkenwell* it is stated that he was buried at Ware, but there is no record of the exhumation in the Clerkenwell Register and no entry of burial in that of Ware. His father's burial at Ware, however, is not recorded in that register, and though the presence of the second large leaden coffin in the vault in St. Mary's chapel would perhaps be in favour of the fact that the son rests by the father, yet where a vault has been admittedly violated, too much stress cannot be laid on such a coincidence.

Pink states, but on what authority I do not know, that the second baronet was "said to have been deprived of his hearing and at length of his speech and to have died unmarried." Northampton Street, which lies east of the north end of St. John's Road some 400 yards n.e. of the church, was originally called Wood's Close; early in the XVIII. century a well known asylum managed by a Dr. Newton was situated in it; and quite possibly a similar institution existed there at the end of the XVII. century. A very charming picture of "Sr Richard Fanshaw Kn^t^," in his early youth, was engraved by Harding in 1792, from the original portrait, by Lely, in possession of — Blount, Esq. (which no doubt had belonged to Christopher Blount, the second Baronet's brother in law). Though the younger Sir Richard was never Knighted, he was again described as *K^t^*, not Bart., in his burial

Register. His father was of mature years before Lely began to paint in England, and had reached the age of 52 when he received the honour of Knighthood, it is therefore impossible that the portrait could have represented the first Baronet.

Plate glass from the coffin of Sir Richard Fanshawe
(see page 222)

Valence House is the home of the London Borough of Barking and Dagenham's Museum and Archives & Local Studies Centre. It is a focus for local community heritage projects in which professional staff encourage enthusiastic volunteers to use their natural talents and learnt skills for mutual benefit.

On the recent closure of the Friends of Valence House, they generously presented a book scanner and purchased a set of ISBN numbers towards the setting-up of Valence House Publications. This is a volunteer-led project with the twin aims of issuing new editions in print and e-book format of rare and out-of-print books from the extensive Valence House collection, together with occasional original publications.

The staff and the resources of Valence House Museum and Archives have made this publication possible, together with the work of the following volunteers: Derek Alexander, Kelly Alexander, Matt Benjamin and Deirdre Marculescu.

www.ingramcontent.com/pod-product-compliance
Ingram Content Group UK Ltd.
Pitfield, Milton Keynes, MK11 3LW, UK
UKHW062304290726
14090UKWH00017B/871